ANGER

ANGER

PSYCHOLOGY
PHYSIOLOGY
PATHOLOGY

By

FREDERIC R. STEARNS, M.D.

CHARLES C THOMAS • PUBLISHER
Springfield • Illinois • U.S.A.

Published and Distributed Throughout the World by
CHARLES C THOMAS • PUBLISHER
Bannerstone House
301-327 East Lawrence Avenue, Springfield, Illinois, U.S.A.
Natchez Plantation House
735 North Atlantic Boulevard, Fort Lauderdale, Florida, U.S.A.

This book is protected by copyright. No part of it
may be reproduced in any manner without written
permission from the publisher.

© *1972, by* CHARLES C THOMAS • PUBLISHER

ISBN 0-398-02612-2

Library of Congress Catalog Card Number: 72-81718

With THOMAS BOOKS careful attention is given to all details of manufacturing and design. It is the Publisher's desire to present books that are satisfactory as to their physical qualities and artistic possibilities and appropriate for their particular use. THOMAS BOOKS will be true to those laws of quality that assure a good name and good will.

Printed in the United States of America
ROO-2

For Ann Mary Stearns

PREFACE

"Recuerdo que una vez me pasé sobre el microscopio veinte horas seguidas avizorando los gestos de un leucocito moroso, en sus labores forcejecos para evadirse de un capilar sanguineo." — "I remember that I once spent twenty continuous hours at the microscope watching the movements of a laggard leucocyte in his struggling efforts to escape from a blood capillary."

Santiago Ramon y Cajal (1)

"The eternal mystery of the world is its comprehensibility."
Albert Einstein (2)

IN my previously published monograph dealing with the psychomatic problem of laughing, it was pointed out that many more of these "minor," though ubiquitous, medical problems exist, problems which heretofore have not been subject to penetrating investigation. One reason is, of course, that these phenomena are neither incapacitating nor life-threatening and are, therefore, not under the social pressure of research demands. Another reason may be their self-evidence as an unquestionable occurrence in everyone's daily life. It seems to us, however, that such "self-evidence" should arouse scientific misgivings in accord with Descartes' tenet: Cogito, ergo sum (I doubt, therefore I exist). We will see, in considering the psychological-physiological-pathological implications of the anger response, that we are dealing not with a self-evident phenomenon but a very complex and intricate one which, notwithstanding its ubiquitousness, is definitely and consistently delimited, standing out as a distinct psychological and physiological function. In a similar fashion, as

1. Ramon y Cajal, S.: *Recuerdo de mi Vida,* 3rd ed. Vol. II, p. 171.
2. *Out of My Later Years.*

we have become aware in investigating laughing, we have found that this "minor" problem of anger ultimately involves the entire human organism, not only as a normal psychosomatic reaction but also as a symptom of abnormal conditions of the human organism. This may permit the conclusion that in medical research there are no "minor" problems.

FREDERIC R. STEARNS, M. D.

CONTENTS

	Page
Preface	vii

Chapter
1. DEFINITION AND PSYCHOLOGY 3
2. PHYSIOLOGY 13
3. PATHOLOGY 17
4. EVALUATION 35
5. COMMENT 50

References 57
Index 67

ANGER

1

DEFINITION AND PHYCHOLOGY

ANGER is one of the most frequent psychosomatic phenomena, one which is experienced by everyone on numerous occasions. Although anger is a well-apprehended and discerned sensation — always reactive, it has never been precisely defined. In the literature, in most instances its properties have been taken for granted; in other instances it may have been mentioned in conjunction with hostility, aggression, and rage; or it has been vaguely differentiated from anxiety and fear.

English and English (1) define anger as an "emotional reaction" aroused by specific stimuli; although they enumerate the stimuli, they do not describe the characteristics of the anger phenomenon which they consider a "passing emotional disturbance." Eccles (2) points to the fact that anger, the psychological peculiarities of which remain unexplained, may become a conscious experience without one's awareness of the explicit stimulus; anger is presented as an example of "the private observation of one's selfconsciousness." Whitehead (3), a philosopher, explains anger as a "feeling ... clearly entwined with the primitive function of 'retreat from.'" Fischer (4) depicts anger "as an increased affective sensitivity" (which is a tautology). Sullivan (5), in his singularly descriptive fashion, contributed an exposition referring to anger: "Sometimes the development of the situation is such that the possibility of any easy resolution of the situation, any reasonable prompt satisfaction of need or elevation of self is contradicted by elements of the situation."

Wolf (6) calls attention to the frequent distinction of emotion and feeling state. He stresses that anger is an emotion (a "psychosomatic manifestation").

Karl Menninger (7) has given a relevant description of anger, although he does not use this caption: "One of the first evidences of failure of the 'normal' devices of the ego for handling emergencies is the development or persistence of stress awareness. The subject is conscious of discomfort in connection with efforts at concentration and self-control. Aware of this, he consciously exerts an extra increase of 'will power' in the mastery or concealment of these phenomena. . . . Less uncomfortable, because unconscious, is the greatly increased use of repression. Externally, this appears as restriction and increased inhibition . . . . Utilizing of these devices of a first degree emergency is nearly always a transient . . . phase (8).

Kubie (9) differentiates between conscious processes of conduct and unconscious processes: "The conduct which is determined by conscious processes is flexible and realistic . . . can be influenced by conscious appeals to reason and feeling, by argument and exhortation . . . has the capacity to learn by experience. . ." (this may be applied to anger responses) but . . . behavior which is determined by unconscious processes is rigid. . . . It never learns from experience, cannot be altered by argument, reason, persuasion. . ." (this may be characteristic of neuroses).

Frank (10) points to the selectivity of emotional reaction and the feedback situation which may be found in anger. "The emotional reaction . . . may operate to increase the sensitivity and selectivity of the organism to certain 'To whom it may concern' messages, internally and also externally. This selectivity is a process of discriminative acceptance or absorption and of response to message. However, the pattern of response is usually a function of past experience and, therefore, may be more or less relevant and appropriate to the message as interpreted, accepted and reacted to. . . . We are faced with a feedback situation which is the dynamic process of interaction: the organ system, the organism-personality has a selective threshold with discriminating acceptance-rejection and patterned responses which is continually operating in the interaction of the responding organ or agent with the environment." This somewhat sophisticated elaboration means simply that only selective ("To whom it may concern") stimuli will initiate emotional responses such as anger responses, which are feedback responses, as past experience is involved.

Lehmann (11) introduces the concept of entropy into emotional responses: "If . . . information input becomes greater than entropy, the result is . . . disruption of time sense and orderly remembering." This is an observation sometimes encountered in anger responses.

Etymologically, the English word "anger" is derived from the old Norse word "angre," which means affliction (Latin: ad-fligere = to strike at). In German, "Ärger" is the noun of "arg," which means wicked; "Ärger," therefore, is the emotional response to "wicked" stimuli. In Spanish, "enojar" (to get angry) derives from "en" and "ojo" — something which offends the eye; the noun "enojo," therefore, also signifies disgust. Another Spanish term for anger is "enfado," which simply refers to trouble. In French, sometimes "chagrin" (from the old French "graignier") translates our anger. More to the point is "dépit," which corresponds to displeasure. Etymology if often an aid to dynamic psychology. In all of these languages, anger is a well-delimited concept and response to an offending stimulus. In none of these languages is the term associated with hostility, aggression, or rage. Essentially, the term in all the cited languages confers uneasiness, displeasure, and resentment.

In order to come closer to the definition of the anger response, we should consider the process of frustration which, in many instances, is an inherent feeling modality of anger. Frustration most often results from environmental pressue of stress. Brown (12) emphasizes that this kind of frustration which is not the result of an "endopsychic conflict" does not cause "a neurotic defense reaction." It is obviously associated with anger response. To assess the degree of frustration (Karl Menninger — reference 7 — thought that a measure of frustration would be desirable), clinical psychologists developed the concept of frustration tolerance (13). Above the tolerance, anger may become a conscious phenomenon.

Kaplan and Goodrich (14) consider frustration involved in anger responses. Jerslid (15) has pointed out that a person is likely to be "angry with himself" if he fails to live up to his expectation, which is only another expression for frustration.

We are not in agreement with Yacorzynski (16), who contends that anger is an "approach to attack the threatening stimulus." Anger is, in most instances, not a reaction to a "threatening" stimulus (which might be fear or hostility) and, thus, is not an "approach to attack" — meaning an abortive aggression.

How, then, can anger be defined? Negatively, it is not hostility or aggression; Abrahamson (17) corroborated this. He explains anger, and the possibility to express it, as a sign of emotional maturity, whereas hostility and hate characterize emotional immaturity. This means that anger and hostility belong to different categories of emotional reactions. He also, elsewhere in his book, differentiates between constructive anger "based on realism" and hostility "based on immature feelings of fear." Anger may be best described as a combination of uneasiness, discomfort, tenseness, resentment (which is a response to selective stimuli), and frustration. The stimuli are manifold. Most of them are informative communications (see below) which are provoking or thwarting; some are recall of, or associations with, such informative communications; others are external physical stimuli (noise — reference 18, touch, etc.). Still others are proprioceptive stimuli (hormonal imbalance: e.g. stress engendered by thyroid or adrenal-cortical hormones — references 19, 20, 21): hunger, fatigue (22), hypoglycemia (23) — hypoglycemia is followed by increased secretion of epinephrine and adrenal steroids.

It may be appropriate here to insert Ashley Montagu's (24) interesting and well-evidenced statement that the same stimulus may initiate different responses, e.g. the identical situation may make one person angry and another person afraid, or the same stimulus may arouse varying degrees of anger in different individuals. His further averment that the same stimulus may evoke different combinations of emotions in different persons — i.e. much anger and little fear or much fear and little anger — cannot be confirmed by this author. Anger is a very well delimited emotional reaction. Any additional emotional response would eliminate the anger response. Anger can, on the other hand, either subside or be repressed, and it can be replaced by emotional reactions such as anxiety, depression, hostility, or aggression. The confusion should be eliminated — namely that, for instance, fear may be a constituent of anger. Fear can replace anger when the informative communication (verbal stimulus), which originally caused the anger response, is rationalized as to its determinant contents; the same may take place when the anger response is supplanted by hostility or aggression.

The attempted definition and delimitation of the anger response is somewhat simplified here and is, in reality, more complex both from the perspective of consciousness as well as "psychological time."

As to consciousness, Eccles (2) has stated that "one can have awareness of being angry... by direct apprehension apart from sensory perception." This apparently means that the stimuli of the anger response are often not distinctly perceived, depending on the nature of the stimuli. He also stresses that in an emotional state like anger there is a specific awareness of self. This, indeed, seems to be one of the essential psychological factors in anger response.

Anger can be both suppressed and repressed. If suppressed, it lingers on consciously and may become converted into motor or sensory manifestations (restlessness, headache). If repressed (secondary repression) — as a defense mechanism, the anger response becomes excluded from awareness; a distorted "symptom formation" (25) may be the result, or the anger may any time emerge into consciousness when recent occurrences create situations associated with the original repression of the stimulus response.

Another phenomenon is forgetting (repressing) the specific stimulus of the anger response, whereas the anger response persists consciously. The duration of this forgetting varies; however, whenever the stimulus is recalled, the anger response generally is attenuated and slowly subsides. Jersild (15) has pointed to the phenomenon of "displaced anger." When there is a situation which prevents the individual from expressing anger toward the offending stimulus (person, situation), he may direct the anger toward someone or something else. Displacement is a common emotional process and is particularly frequent in dreams. Menninger (8) coined the concept of "sublimated anger" and quoted Martin Luther, who stated: "When I am angry... my whole temperament is quickened, my understanding sharpened." This coincides with Abrahamson's (17) classification of anger within emotional maturity and the Russian Pavlovian psychologists who consider anger a "positive emotion."

The time element in the anger response has relevance. Menninger (7) has correctly stated that "any specific feeling has a certain rate of acceleration and deceleration in the process of being built up and fading out." He adds that a biological individuality prevails in this time rate — as in some persons, specific feelings linger for a considerable period, while in others they pass rapidly. French investigators have found that frustration, which is a constituent of the anger response, is "manifested ... by the consciousness of the obstacle, that is, by the time interval." Hence, the unexpected conclusion: When time becomes a conscious reality, it appears too long (26, 27).

This time element in anger response is particularly well demonstrated when waiting is the stimulating situation. Cohn (28) has called this emotional time element "avoidance gradients during waiting," expressing the observation that in concentrating increasingly on the duration of waiting, our uneasiness and discomfort increase as we — more and more — avoid impressions of our environment. Fraisse (27) should best be quoted literally: "In becoming conscious of duration, we also become conscious of resistance." The word duration comes from the Latin "durus" (hard); this double meaning is still apparent in the verb "endure." The resistance is manifested in the form of an emotional state which corresponds to our assessment of the value of the obstacle. . . . Waiting is one of the principal situations in which consciousness of duration spontaneously appears. The result is dissatisfaction and tension.

The most primitive feeling of frustration in the anger response arises from a stimulus of temporal origin: duration. The fact that frustration is a frequent component of anger response is very clearly demonstrated in the waiting situation. If we consider the anger-causing stimuli from infancy to adulthood, carefully avoiding those stimuli which may prompt hostility and aggression, we will, for the present, include only those psychological and physiological stimuli which are not wholly, or part of, pathophysiological and pathopsychological conditions.

In infants, "anger is the most common emotional reaction." Stimuli are "interference with movements," ". . . putting on his clothes when he wants to play," ". . . thwarting some wish — as being picked up," "... having property taken away," etc. (29, 30). Goodenaugh (31) touches upon the anger response in babies and emphasizes that "in an angry outburst the energy is not directed toward any serviceable end." This is a rather trite statement, considering the mental and central nervous system development in babies. However, it is essential that the expression of the anger response in babies is automatically motor and apparently due to subcortical discharges ("in a random fashion") and not relatively fixed and scant in motion as in adults.

In children, the frequency of anger responses reaches its culmination point in the second year of life. There is an increase of motor and verbal resistance (see Goodenaugh, reference 31).

The stimuli which produce anger responses in adolescents differ from those in childhood; they are prevailingly social in nature: teasing, unfairness, lying, bossiness, sarcasm, failing in accomplishments. Generally, the duration of anger response in adolscents is longer than in children (32). In late adolescence the predominant stimuli are "Thwarting of self-assertion and restraints on desires, unjust accusations, insulting comments, unwelcome advice," and interruption of activities (33, 34). After late adolescence, the essential stimuli of the anger response remain more or less unchanged; however, some "threats that arouse fear in the young, arouse anger in the older." Yet, anger continues to be evoked by "thwarting of activities or intentions and assault on self-esteem" (15). Kaplan and Goodrich (14) stress particularly the factor of intention, i.e. that thwarting or provocation perceived as being inflicted against intentions or designs are primary stimuli of anger response in the adult.

Anastasia and associates (35) in an interesting statistical study, found that 52 per cent of anger responses were due to thwarted plans; the interfering agents which comprised this percentage consisted of individuals in 131 cases; institutional factors in 65; accidents, chance factors, and malfunctioning objects in 89; and organic needs or conditions (sleep, illness) in 22. The second most frequent stimuli causing anger response, in 20.9 per cent of the tested individuals, were situations of inferiority and loss of prestige. Anger response promoted by studies occurred in 12.7 per cent, by family difficulties in 9.9 per cent, and by intolerence or cheating in 4.5 per cent. It hardly requires an explanation that recall ("a process by which a representation of past experiences is elicited" — reference 1) of stimuli which have caused an anger response again may have the same effect.

If the original stimulus has been repressed, it is possible that the response comes to the fore in dreams. The anger response corresponds to the dreamer's real attitude." In some however, the response is not anger "but the opposite" Carl Jung who stressed that in some instances the ...t is identical with the conscious anger response, but ...ized that more often there is a "displacement of ...n dreams."

...have considered the stimuli of anger response to c......de with that type of stimuli which we have called elsewhere "informative communication (37)," at least in the adolescent and adult. The fact that the basic conditions which arouse anger ...he adult remain relatively unchanged throughout life ... assumption that in many cases the anger responses ...ditioned reactions, yet one must remember that there ...es with increasing age (15).

... second type of stimuli are exteroceptive. One of these is ...e. Canfield, among others (38, 39, 40), has pointed out that "a sudden noise or a prolonged noise will incite affective conditions which may appear ... as ... anger." Saltzman (41) defines noise as discordant sounds which have no definite pitch. Wolf has evidenced that it is not difficult to quantify the sound input; however, the response (including the anger response) changes from person to person or even from time to time in the same person. He adds that the stimulus gains its force from its meaning. This is rarely so when noise is the stimulus of an anger response. Later in this book we will embark more thoroughly on the physiological effects of noise in their relationship to anger response.

It has been common experience that, under certain conditions, touch may induce an anger response. Unlike noise, where the mere auditory sensation is the stimulus, in the case of touch a specific meaning or significance has, indeed, to characterize the sensation. Thus, touch is in most instances only the means by which an informative communication is conveyed — and, for this purpose, by which a tactile contact of very short duration is established. This also will be dealt with in detail. Sudden visual perception of light, if unexpected and particularly when changing a stable situation (sleep, meditation, concentration), may also serve as a stimulus of an anger response. It is generally not associated with an informative communication unless the light source is set intentionally by persons or avoidable circumstances. It was also reported by Peterson (42) that during heat waves, the tendency to anger responses increases (he ascribes this to the lowered pH during heat waves).

As regards proprioceptive stimuli which may cause anger responses, one may mention Gates' (22) observations and those by Young (43), who found that people are more easily angered when they are hungry and/or tired. In this connection, we may also point to the finding of Gellhorn (23) that individuals with recurrent episodes of hypoglycemia are prone to anger responses. Stratton (44), without analyzing his statement in detail, averred that adults who have a history of severe or protracted childhood illness tend to be "somewhat more subject to anger than persons who had no history of serious childhood illness."

It is generally acknowledged that the female cycle just before and during menstruation increases the predisposition to anger responses. This is particularly true in women who suffer from premenstrual tension. Similarly, many individuals who have chronic constipation are known to have a tendency to anger responses. We have already alluded to the fact that hormonal imbalance (thyroid, adrenal-cortical hormones – reference 19, 20, 21) may augment the disposition to anger responses. We shall revert to these observations in the following chapters.

Selye's (45) concept of stress, especially the vaguely defined denotation of nonspecific stress inasmuch as the nervous system is concerned, differentiates between mild and severe stress. Mild stress as a stimulus produces an "alarm reaction" in which the "most characteristic change is tension" (with predominance of the adrenergic system). "During the stage of resistance, most of these (tension) manifestations disappear, although a certain degree of sympathetico-tonus persists." This description parallels the connotation of anger response expressed in nonpsychological terms. In a later book (46), Selye states in a quite concise way "Mental stressors (orders, challanges, offenses) are met with complex emotional defense responses, which can be summed up as the attitude of 'not being done in'."

2

PHYSIOLOGY

IN the medical literature are scattered reports of the physiological phenomena which are characteristic of, or associated with, the anger response.

The investigations of Wolf and Wolff (47, 48) have been partly confirmed. It appears, according to the last comprehensive paper by Wolf (49), that in the anger response the volume of saliva and the quantity of hydrochloric acid secreted by the stomach are increased, this increase constituting a cholinergic (parasympathetic) stimulation and the gastric mucosa becomes a "hyperemic and engorged." This may well be a sympathetically piloted reaction, though it is probably a sympathetic cholinergic vasodilatation as found in skeletal muscles. It is a recognized fact that "the hypothalamus contains central mechanisms essential in the integrated expression of feline anger." It was recently reported that stimulation of the hypothalamus causes signs of "angry . . . behavior," which also prompts muscular vasodilatation "mediated by cholinergic sympathetic vasodilator fibers" (50). We refer to the possibility of sympathetic involvement in gastric vasodilatation, particularly, because there is no convincing evidence that vasodilator fibers "course in the vagi to the vessels of the thoracic and abdominal viscera." This ambivalence in autonomic nervous innervation can also be observed when nausea accompanies the anger response. There is considerable increase in saliva secretion but almost no hydrochlorid acid secretion. Thus, it appears that in anger response, both parasympathetic and sympathetic discharges are operative in the stomach (52).

It is interesting, as regards our subject, that the observations of Wolf and Wolff have found opponents. Beaumont (53), 111 years before their publication, had already reported inhibition of gastric secretion in anger. Beaumont's report was confirmed by Hornborg (54), Bogen (55), and Schrottenbach (56), 70 to 90 years after

Beaumont's publication. Still, in 1938, McGregor (57) stated, in contradiction to Mittelmann and Wolff (58) and Wolf and Wolff (48), that "minor shades of feeling" also arrested gastric peristalsis and secretion. All in all, we feel that the conclusion reached by Ivy and associates (59) — "that certain emotions may be associated with hypermotility and hypersecretion is suggestive but, by no means, conclusive" — is correct. This statement does not refute the observations by Wolf and Wolff, but emphasizes their ambivalent character so that both parasympathetic and sympathetic discharges may influence the gastric function in the anger response.

Selye (45) has demonstrated that under the influence of anger, the heart rate increases rapidly. As this response is not prevented by denervation of the heart (vagus), the tachycardia is "presumably mediated through liberation of adrenergic hormone," i.e. through sympathetic discharges.

Smirk (60) has set forth that even mild stimuli causing emotional reactions, such as anger responses, may eventually produce blood pressure elevation, and that frequent recurrences of such emotional reactions and hypertensive episodes may "predispose the subject toward the development of essential hypertension." This observation has been confirmed by many investigators and clinicians.

Selye (45) already has reported that in animal experiments, emotional stress is followed by an absolute decrease of lymphocytes in the circulating blood. This, according to Selye, was also observed in man. Lymphocytopenia was found in "stress interviews" in normal persons (61). On the other hand, in psychoneuroses, e.g. in "hysteria" of women, the lymphocyte count is often normal (62).

As a stress interview in a normal individual may have the same effect as a mild alarm reaction in the general adaptation syndrome, i.e. secretion of corticotropin and corticoids, the decrease in the number of lymphocytes in the blood is understandable (63). It is also evident that a "stress interview" belongs in the category of informative communications that frequently produce an anger response. Cardon and Miller (64) reported elevation of free fatty acids in the blood of individuals during anger response. In animal experiments (guinea pigs and rats), it was found that in alarm reactions of the general adaptation syndrome, fatty acid mixtures cause enlargement of the adrenal cortex, so that the ACTH could have a controlling influence on the fat metabolism via cortical steroids (65). Whether these animal experiments have any connection with Cardon and Miller's report (the only one of its kind detected in the medical literature) is highly hypothetical.

While the physiological findings in the anger response are relatively scarce, it is gratifying that much emphasis has been placed on electroencephalographic abnormalities.

Heath (66, 67) has described a patient who had an anger response on recall of "bad memories." He found high amplitude spindling activity in the hippocampus (EEG was performed with a stereotaxic instrument to implant the electrodes and perfusion canule accurately).

In emotionally well balanced adults, theta rhythms are rarely present, but they may be produced by a disagreeable stimulus, particularly if the individual feels thwarted by some personal disrespect. In a French experimental study, a student was stroked by a young lady. An interruption of the stroking prompted a transient appearance of theta rhythms of 6 cycles per second (cps). This seems to evidence that withdrawal of "mildly pleasant" sensations created a response of anger-frustration. This EEG phenomenon was also observed in other individuals who experienced experimental thwarting — i.e. whenever a pleasant situation was intentionally terminated, the theta waves appeared regularly after a few seconds, culminated within about ten seconds, and then gave way to a normal alpha rhythm (68, 69, 70).

Metcalf (71, 72, 73) pointed to the observation that patients with positive spikes frequently exhibit protracted anger directed toward persons who thwarted their intentions or actions. He found bursts of spikes, positive in polarity and with a maximum in the posterior temporal area; the spikes were of the slow type, from 6 to 8 cps.

Strauss (74) — who does not recognize the term "theta rhythm," but includes all slow cycles in the delta rhythm — observed that apprehensiveness and experimentally evoked embarrassment (both often components of the anger response) produce a sharp depression of alpha activity, which is replaced by low voltage random frequency. Similar slowings of the alpha rhythm in anger responses have been reported by Delay (75), Oberman (76), and Wilson (77).

Penfield and Jasper (78), although not specifically referring to anger, have reported that theta rhythm (4 to 7 cps, or even 2 to 4 cps) seems to occur in conditions of aggression and in children with behavior disorders. This may well include anger response, considering the autonomic motor anger response in small children and the frequent confusion in delimiting anger response from aggression and hostility. The authors could not provoke "anger" by electrical stimulation of the cortex. This is understandable, as it is assumed that theta waves (the brain potentials represented in anger response) originate in the subcortical ganglia and not in the cortex.

In a more general way, Walter (79) has set forth that theta rhythm (4 to 7 cps) is "sometimes associated with emotional activity."

In the Kinsey report (80) it is stated that "frustrated sexual responses" in the female turn into anger. The report continues to parallel the physiological profile of this "sexual syndrome" with that of anger: increase in pulse rate and blood pressure, sometimes vasodilatation, increase in peripheral blood circulation, probably adrenalin secretion, increase in muscular tension; but there are differences. There is increase in surface temperature in the female "sexual syndrome," which has not been reported in anger response.

3

PATHOLOGY

A NOT too infrequent complaint of individuals who experience an anger response is headache. The term "tension headache," although not precisely defined, hardly applies to this type of headache. Tension headache has been described as a somatic reaction (dilatation of cerebral vessels) to recurrent stress of long standing. It has been depicted most often as a severe throbbing pain of considerable duration. Headache which is felt in anger responses resembles more closely the "psychogenic" headache, which has been described by various authors as a pressure at the top of the head, pain in the scalp, or as a "band" about the head — occassionally localized in the front, vertex, or back of the head. It is always of relatively short duration and subsides after the anger response has disappeared. This headache may be due to muscular contraction of face and head muscles (81).

Fischer (4) mentions in passing that after brain concussion, the patient — especially when disturbed during sleep or when interviewed or physically examined — often demonstrates an anger response (reference 4, p. 114). The same author stated that disturbances of impulse, as sometimes present after encephalitis or in patients with injuries to the frontal lobe, in whom the intellectual capacities have remained within normal test limits, may try to overcome the lack of impulse "by deliberately putting themselves in a state of anger." This may be due to an adrenergic mechanism consequent to a thwarting stimulus. After prefontal lobotomy, Rylander (82) reported the observation of "affective incontinence," which (in this context) means to respond with anger to rather trivial occurrences.

Freeman and Watts (83) remark in this respect that after prefontal lobotomy, the patients retain the capacity of displaying appropriate emotional responses, but the responses are evoked more easily, lacking depth, and are "quite transitory." This description fits that of some anger responses. Anger after prefontal lobotomy also was reported when the patient was confronted with concrete test material which could be seen and handled (e.g. sorting test).

According to Tow (84), it is possible that in these patients, the recall of a more successful preoperative performance could engender an anger (anger-frustration) response. The response was particularly distinct in applying the maze test; errors would prompt an anger response (85, 86, 87).

Henrichs et al (88) observed emotional complications after open heart surgery; among others, anger response was prevalent. Women were less affected that men. In cardiac diseases, in general, anxiety plays the foremost role psychosomatically. There has been found only one suggestion in the medical literature that "troublesome events in day-to-day experiences (among which are anger responses) may precipitate arrhythmias, including paroxysmal atrial tachycardia, extrasystoles and ... paroxysmal ventricular tachycardia" (89).

As to the endocrine system in relation to anger response, there are numerous reports in the literature. Anger responses may occur in thyroid hormone imbalance. This is particularly true in mild hyperthyroidism in which there is a predominance of the sympathetic nervous system with tachycardia, perspiration and fine tremor.

McGavack (90) has pointed out that a neurohormonal mechanism is involved which causes nervous impulses to pass with considerably increased frequency and intentsity via the hypothalamus to the anterior pituitary gland; the output of the thyrotropic (or thyroid-stimulating) hormone is increased. This excessive output of thyroid hormone produces secondary effect throughout the body. The suppressive effect of the thyroid hormone upon the secretion of the thyrotropic hormone by the anterior pituitary gland does not suffice to neutralize the strong nervous stimulation originating in the hypothalamus. It thus appears that the frequently observed anger response (McGavack himself states "A trifling annoyance will anger him greatly") is secondary to the sympathetic discharges initiated in the hypothalamus.

It is well known, of course, that in massive overproduction of thyrotropic and thyroid (thyrotoxin) hormones, such as in Graves' disease, more intense emotional disturbances may appear which may culminate in frank psychoses. In myxedema, the generally observed indolence is sometimes interrupted by episodes of aggression or rage, but there is never a typical anger response. The aggressive episodes may lead to "myxedematous psychosis," which often is ameliorated by administration of thyroid hormone. The neurological etiology remains obscure, but there is certainly not a sympathetic discharge operative, which most frequently is associated with the anger response (91).

In Addison's disease it has been reported that with progression of the ailment, the patient becomes moody and emotionally unstable, so that anger responses to adequate stimuli can be anticipated (20). As hypoglycemia is a frequent finding in Addison's disease, accompanied by an increased secretion of epinephrine and adrenal-cortical hormones, this may be the physiological basis of the anger responses. It is also interesting that the EEG in Addison's disease in many cases exhibits an interruption of the normal alpha rhythm by slow waves, resembling delta waves, the type we have above depicted as characteristic in anger response (93).

In acromegaly (and gigantism), anger responses have been reported, particularly in the early stages. These anger responses have been interpreted in various ways. One explanation is merely psychological: The resentment due the progressive physical deformity gives rise to adequate stimuli to anger response. Yacorzynski (16) is of the opinion that hyperpituitarism "affects the brain in many diverse ways, so that behavioral changes may not actually be due to direct action of the hormones but to their indirect metabolic conditions in general." This is a statement which begs the question. Talbot et al (94) point out that adult acromegalics "may show evidence of excess thyrotropic and adrenotropic hormone in addition to signs of excess growth hormone." Here, again, may be the link to occasional sympathetic discharges upon specific stimuli.

It was already set forth that essential hypertension — though emotional factors are not chiefly causative — may become temporarily aggravated by anger responses. This was reported by

Cannon (95), and has since then been confirmed by many investigators.

The association of allergic reactions and emotions is a well-known fact. In most cases, anxiety and depression are the trigger impulses. There is only one definite instance mentioned in the medical literature in which an anger response (called there "frustration and resentment") was responsible for a nasal allergic phenomenon. First alluded to by Proetz (96), it was later experimentally and clinically confirmed by Holmes and co-workers (97). After primary swelling of the nasal mucosa the hyperemia subsides and is replaced by a pale nasal edema.

Wolff (98), in a later paper, stressed that various individuals react with preference in specific areas; he distinguishes between "stomach reactors," "nose reactors," pulse reactors," and others. Hack (99), at the end of the 19th century, pointed out that functional as well as allergic nasal reactions were due to reflex disturbances. Hansel (100) indicated that "when the nose is in a state of hypersensitiveness, the sensory as well as the sympathetic and parasympathetic systems are hyperirritable."

Lederer (101) also emphasized that "it is theoretically possible, that every single symptom observed as a result of an allergic disease could be elicted in the absence of immunoreactions by selective stimulation of the proper autonomic fibers." The same author deals with the role of emotional disorders in the causation of allergic disorders. He is somewhat evasive in his acceptance of the emotional factor but admits that "stress and strain can cause pronounced changes in the biological balance of both nonallergic and allergic individuals. In the latter, however, the disturbed equilibrium tends to find its somatic expression in an increased responsiveness of the shock tissues to specific and nonspecific stimuli .." "in other words, the allergic individual becomes an allergic patient." This is a rather noncommittal statement.

Ashley (102) was more specific; he contended that "in allergic reactions the normal sympathetic-parasympathetic balance is disturbed and that generally the parasympathetic system prevails over the sympathetic system. This, however, has not been proved satisfactorily." Yacorzynski (16) points to the frequent mention of underlying emotional factors in allergies. He compares "the biochemical changes to those of the alarm reaction" in the general adaptation syndrome, but "the mechanism involved is not yet known."

All of this does not consistently explain why with some nasal allergy cases, anger responses are associated. It appears that an adequate stimulus for a short period of time produces the sympathetic syndrome of uneasiness, frustration, and tenseness, which distinguishes the anger response. There is also a possibility that epinephrine or ephedrine treatment in allergy stimulates sympathetic discharges. It is well known that among the side effects of ephedrine, apprehension has been reported. Epinephrine may engender even stronger emotional responses, also in the direction of apprehension and tenseness. These adrenergic effects are certainly a fertile soil for occasional anger responses.

Wolff and others (103) described, in patients with acne vulgaris, an abnormal physiological sign occurring in anger response: The sebum output was increased two to five times. It has been evidenced that removal of the adrenal and pituitary glands leads to atrophy of the sebaceous glands so that aside from androgen, the sympathetic division of the autonomic nervous system is involved.

Women entering the menopause frequently display behavior changes. We are not concerned here with the more serious symptoms of depression and anxiety due to the physiological modification of femininity; but without doubt, a majority of these women exhibit emotional instability.

Fluhman (104) states, "there are exaggerations of the patient's former response so that some climacteric women may respond with considerable anger to stimuli which, before onset of the menopause, have evoked no or little anger response." The physiological explanation for the quantitative and qualitative alteration of the anger response is not quite clear.

It is known that in the course of the menopause, there is an increase of gonadotropic hormones in the urine as the ovary gradually becomes refractory to the influence of pituitary hormones. Estrogens, on the other hand, are rarely found in the urine. When they are present, it has been assumed that probably the adrenal cortex plays a role in the production of estrogen during and after the menopause. It is also known that during the menopausal period there are "sporadic increases of adrenalin secretion" and "the entire nervous system is made hypersensitive to stimuli." Thus, the autonomic nervous system is responsible for the endocrine changes during the menopause (105).

Crossen cites Maranon (106), who "found that many of the indefinite symptoms complained of could be traced to hypersecretion of the adrenal gland" and "more recent work has confirmed his clinical observations." We have touched upon these observations in order to adduce some evidence that in the menopausal period, the sympathetic part of the autonomic nervous system becomes quite active, and that the enhanced anger responses may find a physiological basis due to this fact.

In the male climacteric, there may be a similar augmentation of the anger response, but only in a minority of cases. The physiological representation may parallel — applied to the male endocrine system — that of the female climacteric. Again, the assumption is justified that adrenergic discharges may accompany anger responses.

In premenstrual tension, the etiological factor apparently is an abnormality of the water metabolism and retention of sodium ion. Thorn et al (107, 108) have demonstrated these facts and have also observed that with the start of the menstrual flow, water and sodium chloride are increasingly excreted. It is known that some women who experience premenstrual tension exhibit "menstrual edema." Thorn associated water and sodium chloride retention with a considerable increase of the estrogen titer in the premenstrual period.

Whether the adrenal gland is operative in this process has never been proved. However, Morton (109) found that hypoglycemia is a frequent finding and in hypoglycemia, an increased epinephrine production is common. Furthermore, Morton observed trembling of hands, which is found occasionally in sympatheticotonus. Greenhill and Freed (110) have offered the hypothesis that the premenstrual retention of the sodium ion with the concomitant edema also causes a mild cerebral edema, and they ascribe the appearance of the emotional symptoms in premenstrual tension to this assumed occurrence.

A number of authors believe that estrogen-androgen imbalance is coresponsible for the symptoms of premenstrual tension. When we consider that a disturbance of the water metabolism is a principal cause of premenstrual tension, we must remember — without going into details — that the hypothalamus (probably its supraoptic nuclei) has a controlling influence on the secretion of the antidiuretic hormone from the neurohypophysis. The hypothalamus, by way of the posterior pituitary, also influences the uterus, particularly through vasopressor factor, which also has antidiuretic properties.

Whether, indeed, the hypothalamus-posterior pituitary axis via the antidiuretic hormone is a factor in the etiology of the water metabolism disorder in premenstrual tension is a proposition which requires experimental and clinical confirmation. The fact, however, that hypoglycemia may accompany premenstrual tension and that the subsequent increase of epinephrine may be anticipated points to a relation of the hypothalamus and the adrenal gland, which is clearly adrenergic. We, then, would have a stimulation of the hypothalamic centers, both regarding the posterior pituitary and the adrenal gland. It is, of course, an open question whether this physiological mechanism contributes to the neurohumoral representation of an anger response.

Chronic constipation has been reported as a predisposition for anger response. Many organic conditions in which constipation is a symptom must be excluded. Mechanical obstruction of the colon, fecal impaction, cerebrovascular accidents cannot be included. Also, the so-called spastic constipation (111) generally does not belong in this category. The spasticity of the colon muscles are due to parasympathetic discharges and can be relieved by atropine. We are concerned with the hypomotility of the colon which may result from sympathetic irritation, generally classified as atonic constipation (111, 112). Because of the atonicity of the muscles, there is a slow movement of the feces through the colon; this affects reabsorption of water with induration of the feces. Although atonic constipation is not in all cases a pure sympathetic phenomenon, it is so in the majority of cases.

Horner (112) has stressed that in what he calls "central constipation," the cause is "direct stimulation or inhibition of the autonomic nerves." Among other central nervous system centers, he points to the role of the hypothalamus and stresses the influence of emotions on central constipation on the basis of hypothalamic involvement. The chronicity of atonic constipation may be due to continous sympathetic overactivity, which may also be responsible in producing a propensity to anger responses upon adequate stimuli.

Schiff (111) enumerates physical signs often associated with chronic constipation, such as hyperhidrosis, cardivascular instability, and cold hands, all sings of sympathetic irritation. Cannon (113) has already stated that "mild affective states" cause constipation. "The orderliness of the central arrangements is upset"..., "the stronger member of the pair prevails".... "Only on such a basis at present can I offer an explanation for the activity and supremacy of the sacral innervation of the bladder and colon, when the sympathetic innervation is aroused."

From a psychological vantage point, Grace and collaborators (114) have stressed that individuals with chronic constipation exhibit "grim holding on" responses, while individuals with frequent diarrhea display a "riddance" response when they have "lost face" or feel thwarted. This obviously means that "grim holding on" or anger reaction is associated with constipation and a minimizing response is associated with diarrhea. This may be an oversimplification, but it is clinical experience.

Wechsler (115) has pointed to "hysteric constipation,"... "which perhaps is the most common of all symptoms," and which he includes in the visceral hysteric conversion phenomena. However, he does not attempt to give a physiological interpretation. He also does not pinpoint the type, but only suggests "it is probably within the range of the irritable colon," which is distinguished by intermittent constipation. He thus probably refers to spastic constipation, in which, emotionally, anxiety (not anger responses) is the prevailing factor. Neurophysiologically, both the clinical signs and the emotional disorder point to parasympathetic predominance. Although not definitely corroborated by urological and neurological reports, it can be concluded that with predominance of sympathetic discharges in anger response, the renal blood flow and, therewith, the frequency and quantity of micturition is reduced (15).

While in cancer, depression and anxiety are the outstanding emotional reactions, Deitch and Shulkin (116) have found that in the emotional readjustment phase, particularly in disfiguring and/or incapacitating malignancies, anger responses came to the fore which "are common to patients with chronic illness." It has been evidenced that anxiety is essentially due to parasympathetic discharges, which has been demonstrated by Wolf and Wolff (117) after vagotomy. One may be justified to assume that the anxiety-depression syndrome in cancer patients is a parasympathetic representation. Yet, the anger responses which have been observed in the late chronic course in cancer patients have been elicited experimentally by Deitch and Shulkin (116). When depression in cancer patients is managed by administration of sympathomimetic drugs, amine oxidase inhibitors, and compounds such as imipramine or nialamide, particularly when little rapport between physician and patient has been established, anger responses may come to the foreground.

It is possible that the sympathomimetic agents block the parasympathetic discharges, so that the anxiety-depression reaction is for a short peroid of time replaced by sympathetic discharges, engendering anger responses. Whether these anger responses in chronic cancer patients may occur spontaneously is not consistently proved, although there are reports in the literature (especially in the psychoanalytic literature) that anger responses "toward parental figures," as a phenomenon of emotional regression, may ocassionally appear spontaneously.

In the anger responses which are sometimes observed in protracted pulmonary tuberculosis, both psychological dynamics and physiological activities may be operative. Dufault et al (118) point to the emotional trauma which may be caused by the experience of the diagnosis. In most instances this may initiate an anxiety neurosis and "revolt," resulting in "self-centeredness." However, occasionally there are cases in which "pettiness may prevail after prolonged treatment. These are the patients in whom frustration-anger responses may appear.

Psychologically, these anger responses are due in part to the monotony of the environment and the restrictions enjoined on the patients by hospital regulations and the relative isolation.

Physiologically, one must take into account the frequently present low-grade fever, the rapid pulse rate, and the sometimes-occurring night-sweats. We will, briefly and in passing, touch upon these signs, which are not primarily within the scope of our considerations.

We know that the hypothalamus is the essential brain structure controlling the temperature regulation. We are informed by the investigations of Ranson and collaborators (119, 120) that lesions in the dorsolateral hypothalamus produce permanent poikilothermic states. It can be imagined, when toxic protein substances in tuberculosis affect the dorsolateral part of the hypothalamus, that there is a toxic stimulation of the sympathetic center of the hypothalamus. Dubois (121, 122) and others have intimated that due to a feedback mechanism (experiments in animals), increase in heat production accompanies fever.

It is general knowledge that acceleration of the pulse rate is a function of the sympathetic autonomic nervous system and is centrally located in the posterior and lateral centers of the hypothalamus. The main nerve centers which control sweating are also situated in the hypothalamus. The sweat glands are innervated by cholinergic fibers of the sympathetic division of the autonomic nervous system, or by peripheral nerves which carry sympathetic fibers. Stimulation of the sympathetic fibers which engender sweat secretion produce acetylcholine, which is found in the sweat. Night-sweats are by no means pathognomic for pulmonary tuberculosis. They may be explained by the fact that the "typical temperature curve of tuberculosis is normal or subnormal in the morning and elevated in the afternoon or evening" (123). There are exceptions.

At any rate, the frequent symptoms in chronic pulmonary tuberculosis — fever, tachycardia, and night-sweats — are due to sympathetic discharges. This may assist in explaining that in the chronic stage of the disease, upon adequate stimuli, the emotional reactions may be anger responses, which harmonizes with the psychological observations in those cases in which "pettiness" may be the basic mood-coloring during protracted disease.

As to rheumatoid arthritis, Brown and associates (124) have dealt extensively with the involved psychosomatic problems.

Considering the prodromal symptoms, they point to morning fatigue, tension, and anger without adequate cause. They stress that it may take months or years until the final diagnosis is arrived at. The authors also indicate that emotional reactions often are as severe as joint symptoms.

Some authors even have voiced the opinon that "psychologic abnormalities" may play a causative role, rather than a symptomatic part, in rheumatoid arthritis. Brown and associates (124) have emphasized "... it is apparent that cerebral functions is one target of the disease...,furthermore, when rheumatoid remission has occurred, the reduction of psychologic symptoms to an inconsequential level has been a frequent finding." Although depression is a common emotional reaction to pain in rheumatoid arthritis, Brown and collaborators state "Other typical psychologic abnormalities are the tendencies to harbor resentment and to express sudden unreasonable anger." All of these symptoms may improve remarkably with remission, even after having been present for many years.

The authors have little explanation for the emotional reactions in rheumatoid arthritis, particularly the "sudden anger response." On one hand, they point to the causative role of emotional stress; on the other hand they consider the brain as a "target organ" of the rheumatoid process, resulting in disturbed cerebral functions. The authors are inclined, however, to consider a "hypersensitivity mechanism" as a basic component of the rheumatic complex which has been frequently adduced etiologically in the previous reports: ... "psychological abnormalities ... could be explained best by some factor which would relate to cellular metabolism in general. The influence of the reacting substance would provide such a relationship."

All of these hypotheses, although founded on laboratory tests, steroid treatment and withdrawal, seasonal variations, refractory periods, remission in pregnancy, etc., do not explain specifically the cerebral "target areas" whose functional disorder might be responsible for the anger response, which, indeed, is not infrequently observed in the course of rheumatoid arthritis.

Selye (45) has referred to many authors (references listed in his book) who have considered a relationship between the general adaptation syndrome and rheumatoid arthritis; the main emphasis has been placed on changes in the adrenal cortex. Hench and others (125) administered large doses of cortisone or ACTH to patients with rheumatoid arthritis. The dramatic improvement obtained subsided upon discontinuation of these hormones.

It has been asserted that corticosteroid treatment is mainly anti-inflammatory and that the doses should be kept low (126) (in contrast to Hench). We have mentioned this only in order to intimate the possibility of a hypothalamic-anterior pituitary-adreno-cortical axis in rheumatoid arthritis. Harris (127) has pointed particularly to the role of the posterior (sympathetic) region of the hypothalamus in this axis. Selye (45) refers to experimental data which seem to prove that "a derangement of the glucocorticoid: mineralo-corticoid balance was considered to be the cardinal factor."

In which manner the posterior hypothalamus, by the way of its hormonal control and the imbalance of the corticoid hormones, may be involved in the anger responses in rheumatoid arthritis remains an open question, but perhaps worth mentioning because it is the sympathetic area of the hypothalamus which is affected.

We accept Wechsler's (128) designation "apoplectic stroke," as a generalizing term for all forms of cerebrovascular accidents which result in loss of consciousness or in coma. The pathological findings and the signs and symptoms are well known. If the patients survive and regain consciousness, the mental and emotional sequelae, as most authors concur, depend largely on the site and the extent of the cerebral lesion.

Severe disturbances are not rare: memory defects, intellectual defects, occasional delirious conditions, and even actual psychoses. In other instances, after the stuporous state has subsided, the mentality shows hardly any alteration. Yet, cases have been reported in which behavior disorders develop. These are the patients in whom anger responses to adequate or inadequate stimuli color the poststuporous syndrome.

Kraepelin (129) has presented in his lectures case histories in which anger responses were observed in the postapoplectic course. Wechsler (128), in his textbook, states "sometimes he (the patient) shows psychic symptoms, such as . . . anger." Recently,

Fisher and associates (130) have indicated that only few patients in the postcomatose course have serious behavior problems, but that ill temper and peevishness are common. These terms parallel our definition of anger responses.

Because of the varying etiology (hemorrhage, thrombosis, embolism), the different cerebral sites involved, the different preictus personality makeup, the different constitutional types — according to Sheldon (131, 132) and others we do not venture to enter into a discussion of the physiological basis of the anger responses in the postapoplectic phase. It appears, however, that sympathicotonic individuals are more prone to experience cerebrovascular accidents than other constitutional types, and this may be a tenuous clue as to why some of these patients may exhibit anger responses in the extended postapoplectic period.

The behavior in post-traumatic conditions has been investigated throughly, mainly after trauma to the head. The reason is that an involvement of the brain may be anticipated, so that the subsequent behavior pattern might be correlated with major, minor, or even minimal cerebral lesions. This can be suspected when diagnosed brain lesions and altered behavior patterns either coincide or appear post-traumatically. However, in many cases a trauma to the head does not result in clinically evident cerebral damage; yet, there is in these cases a diagnostic category, termed "chronic brain syndrome," although in a number of cases indicative neurological signs are missing or minimal.

On the other hand, after trauma to the head there may be mild functional limitations, which may prompt frustration-anger responses. These responses perhaps can be compared with Goldstein's (133) "slight catastrophic reaction." It occurs as an "equalization process" and is observed "where the . . . course goes beyond a definite or normal limit"; it signifies defective behavior of the organism with danger for its performance capacity.

According to Branch and Cole (134), "the post-traumatic personality includes some infantile demandingness," which is one of the determining factors of anger responses. However, in contrast to the chronic brain syndrome and the post-traumatic syndrome, anger responses in the post-concussion syndrome have been reported very infrequently. One author (135) mentions that the patient with post-concussion syndrome "reacts angrily to noise," but this statement is not well substantiated, as he continues "he jumps at sudden noises," which resembles more a startle pettern than an anger response.

Of course, both in the chronic brain syndrome and in the post-traumatic syndrome — before arriving at the conclusion that anger responses belong to the symptomatology — one must evaluate the pretraumatic behavior pattern, as, not infrequently, anger responses were present before the trauma, particularly in accident-prone individuals.

As to the physiological basis of anger responses in post-traumatic conditions, our knowledge is scarce, to say the least. One can only quote Brosin (136), who stated "With our present lack of information about the physiological dynamics of all stages of head injury and the lack of more precise ways to measure objectively the nature of the anatomical, biochemical, electronic, and related psychological functions, it is difficult to assess judicially the nature of the traumatic process in the individual patient."

Suprisingly, not many psychosomatic reports of post-traumatic conditions, other than head injuries, have been published. One large area which hardly has been touched upon includes amputations after trauma. Thompson (137) has embarked on the mental rehabilitation of amputees and has indicated that the amputee may be "disgruntled and ill tempered," that he may show "resentment toward persons as well as toward his artificial limb." Here we find an obvious depiction of anger responses in somewhat different terms. It is not necessary to adduce additional literature (which is listed in Thompson's chapter), because the enumerated authors have not contributed any additional experiences to Thompson's observation. Yet, Thompson stresses that he has found corroboration by Klopstey and Wilson (138).

No physiological explanation has been forthcoming for anger responses after traumatic amputations. It is not rare that the traumatic event which leads to amputation generally will cause oligemic shock, and that the emergency mechanism which is initiated after oligemic shock is due to sympathetic discharges: rise of pulse rate and rise of respiratory rate. This emergency mechanism will only fail if the blood loss continues. However, if adequate therapy is instituted, the sympathetic autonomic nervous system will remain operative: The blood pressure will rise, the peripheral circulation will be restored, the muscle tone will increase and be normalized. It is possible, though hypothetical, that the sympathetic effect will persist to some extent through and after the recuperation stage, so that the emotional reactions will parallel the physiological predominance of the sympathetic division (139, 140).

One of the more recent but rather frequent traumatic syndromes is whiplash injury, most often observed in automobile collisions. Delayed emotional accompaniments are, among others, tension and mood changes. The late emotional reactions depend on three main factors: One is an actual persistence of painful organic changes of the cervical spine and adjacent tissues, which could explain the tension and mood swings (this occurs, however, only in a minority of cases); the second factor is a neurotic overlay which derives from compensation demands or expectations. Here one finds an aggravation of both somatic and emotional symptoms, which subside spontaneously after the financial compensation has been settled.

Myerson (141) has contended that generally only individuals "predisposed to neurosis" will, after an accident, show signs of compensation neurosis, the main symptom of which is "an increasing resentment." The same observation was reported by Kozol (142). As Kozol has correctly stated, the third factor prompting emotional reactions is the pretraumatic personality makeup. Individuals who have no "neurotic character traits" (1) are not disposed to exhibit late mood changes and tension, particulary when consistently motivated to get well and when they must resume their occupations (farmers, independent businessmen, professionals).

The mood changes and the tension state to which we have referred as delayed or late emotional responses after whiplash injuries may be explained by the fact that in neck injuries the sympathetic division of the autonomic nervous system is predominantly involved. Irritation of the sympathetic ganglia in the neck may produce the usual sympathetic signs such as dilatation of the pupils, dizziness, headache, sweating, tremor, etc., but also, during an irritation of long standing, the emotional reactions of mood swings, tension, and discomfort. It is, therefore, understandable — from a physiological point of view as well — that in delayed or late stages of whiplash injuries, anger responses may become part of the behavior pattern.

A traumatic syndrome may be included, called "reflex sympathetic dystrophy" (post-traumatic dystrophy of the extremities). This syndrome is interesting, because sympathetic discharge signs dominate the picture. After an injury, even a minor trauma, recovery is delayed. Pain is increasing and spreading. There is cutaneous involvement as observed in irritation of the sympathetic nervous system, including sweating, glossiness of skin, and trophic changes. There may follow fibrosis of muscles and even atrophic bone alterations. Mild cases, albeit untreated, usually heal spontaneously. Others may progress both as to pain and vasomotor disturbances.

The prevalance of the sympathetic system is furthermore manifested by tachycardia, general perspiration, and vasomotor imbalance. Emotionally, tension and instability are in the foreground. The etiology of the involvement of the sympathetic nervous system has remained obscure. Neither the irritation of the sympathetic division of the autonomic nervous system nor the original trauma explain satisfactorily the reflex dystrophy. "Very likely some disturbance of the central nervous system is the essential factor, which, moreover, may be closely related to the emotional reaction of these patients" (143, 144). This is not an enlightening statement, but we have here, undoubtedly, an example of a psychosomatic disorder in which sympathetic stimulation prevails, and in which tension and instability characterize the emotional status consistently, a status in which anger responses to adequate stimuli must be anticipated.

In convulsive disorders, some authors do not concur that there exists an "epileptic personality"; they contend that the increased tension (anticipation of seizures) and the tendency to anger responses upon slight and often inadequate stimuli are brought about by the prejudicious attitude toward the epileptic individual who is limited in his education, occupation, and social pursuits (145, 146).

Other authors have voiced the opinion that in chronic convulsive disorders, there is "a constant increase of ... irritability" (147) which, together with other behavior features such as intolerance, inflexibility, pedantry, etc., justifies the assumption of an epileptic personality makeup as the basis of increased anger responses. These authors who adhere to the development of an "epileptic personality" believe that it evolves in the course of organic brain changes: "diffuse microscopic injuries," even in idiopathic epilepsy. At any rate, typical and frequent anger responses can be observed in convulsive disorders yet the question remains open whether thay are due to the effect or due to the cause of the seizures.

Some patients with the ill-defined diagnosis of "psychopathic personality" may respond with anger to trivial and inappropriate stimuli. The psychiatric hypothesis on which this diagnosis is arrived at is that these patients suffer from a "character neurosis" which derives from traumatic early childhood experiences. Of course, the term "character neurosis" is tautological with the term "psychopathic personality," and the interpretation is hardly convincing, as every child has had traumatic emotional experiences. The neurological hypothesis is more or less an analogy of the personality changes which were observed as emotional residuals of the epidemic or lethargic encephalitis epidemic which occurred after World War I (148).

It is conspicuous that the electroencephalograms in a great percentage of these cases are abnormal. Hill and Waterson (149) found abnormal electroencephalograms in 48 per cent of cases. However, lower percentages also have been reported. Simons and associates (150) recorded only 9.2 per cent. The electroencephalographic changes, according to Strauss (74), consist of symmetric, irregular delta activity, 3 to 6 cps, at times even slower. The localization was most often in the anterior areas of the brain. This is the type of electroencephalographic alterations which have been described in anger responses.

Whether psychotomimetic drugs could cause anger responses and thus support experimentally our point of view of sympathic predomenance is still a moot question, particularly as anger response, according to the very astute remark by Wiener (151) is not "a normal pathology, but a pathology of norms." Yet, some of these drugs (e.g. LSD) induce "a central sympathetic excitation" with symptoms which are frequently found in anger response — tachycardia, mydriasis, changed heart rate and blood pressure, and electroencephalographic changes, stimulation of monosynaptic reflexes (e.g. patellar reflex) and of the synapses in the reticular formation which prompt increased sensibility to sensory stimulation (152). It is well known, also, that psychotomimetic drugs in some instances and dosages cause feeling of unpleasantness, resentment, and frustration, all of which are found in anger responses accompanied by sympathetic discharges.

4

EVALUATION

ALL previously enumerated emotional and physiological signs and symptoms of the anger response are overshadowed by a sensory phenomenon in the chest, which is, however, difficult to describe. It is an "unpleasant feeling as alluded to by Montagu (24), who states that "awareness of the operation of the sympathetic system is associated with an unpleasant feeling of an organic tone."

As to the sympathetic afferent nerves, Gillilan (153) pointed out that they "carry impulses which are relayed to higher levels for conscious sensation." He refers particularly to the afferent visceral fibers of the heart, which "reach the spinal cord through the middle and inferior cervical nerves and ganglia." It is also possible that the unpleasant intrathoracic sensation is associated with the accelerated heart rate and the "general instability of the heart" as found in sympatheticotonic constitutional types.

Wolf and Wolff (98, 154) demonstrated a similar observation — namely, that in many persons during periods of stress, the heart function may be altered, as the cardiac output is increased as is the force of muscular contractions "which may give rise to unusual chest sensations." Another factor may be involved in the peculiar intrathoracic sensation in anger response; Wolf (155), too, has pointed to the fact that in response to stress-producing life situations "in association with . . . anger . . . , insufficient pulmonary ventilation may occur." In these reactions, "the diaphragm is flattened, due to increased muscular contractions and shortening." This phenomenon may cause the inability of full inspiration and so may prompt substernal tightness and a feeling "of breathing only with the top of the chest." A less frequent but sometimes observed sensation in anger response is epigastric pressure. The symptom is understandable when one recalls the comprehensive investigations by Wolf and Wolff (47, 48) as described above.

From a psychological descriptive point of view, the anger response is well delimited, as we have already indicated. Some reasons have been brought forth when we touched upon the difinition of anger, its biological development, and even adducing etymology. The identification — often found in the literature — of anger with hostility, aggression, and rage (or, derived from animal experiments: sham rage) is a confusion of issues. This confusion has become very obvious in the attempt by Dembo (156) to experimentally induce an anger response. She confronted individuals with insoluble tasks and observed as reaction "disorganization life space," resulting in escape from the task situation, or in random activities, or in "regression to lower level of activity." She considered this to be an anger response.

Confrontation with an unsoluble problem which soon is recognized as such causes either hostility or humor, but not anger. On the other hand, an individual faced with soluble problems, recognized as soluble, with which he is unable to cope, may cause an anger response with the characteristic components of frustration, resentment, and uneasiness. Here we have a good example of the confusion of hostility or other irritability reactions with a typical anger response. Anger, as Brown (12) clearly observed when analyzing frustration, is not an "endopsychic conflict," but a normal response to stimuli, such as informative communication, including recall as well as exteroceptive and proprioceptive ones as outlined above.

As anger cannot be described conceptually in a single-phased proposition, because it contains psychological and physiological characteristics which, due to the symbolism of language and the compartmentation of our physiological approaches, can only be set forth in analytical sequestration, it has incurred the risk of diffusion and overlapping with disparate concepts. We would like to stress again, however, that the anger response is a consistently confined phenomenon, not only because of its psychological components but also because physiologically the anger response carries a prevailingly sympathetic representation in contradistinction to frequently equalized emotional manifestations, such as hostility, aggression, rage, which have predominantly parasympathetic representations, although the sympathetic nervous system may play a minor role in some of them. We have limited the psychological delineation of anger to five most frequently experienced components: uneasiness, unpleasantness, tenseness, frustration, resentment. Bindra (157) has tried to find a uniform denominator for the anger response which contains some constructive ideas, but, on the whole, it is not elucidating. He contends that emotions such as anger have a "common construct": a "central motive state," which is "a set of neural processes arising from an interaction of a certain type of physiological state and a certain class of incentive stimuli."

We are dealing, thus, with "a neural functional change" occurring through interaction of a physiological state and incentive stimuli. The neural changes "favor selective attention" to certain incentive stimuli and also "create a response bias." Altogether, the denominator of "interaction of a physiological state and incentive stimuli" is somewhat vaguely condensed in the term "central motive state." If this denominator would be bolstered by clearly substantiated physiological facts, the attempt of a uniform interpretation may have had some merit. However, the way in which the problem is approached leads us to the impression of a very superficial and hazy hypothesis.

Eccles (2), who was quoted above, made the pertinent remark that in the anger response, the awareness of self is particularly characteristic; in spite of the peculiarity of the stimuli involved, according to Eccles, the anger response is less a special response to a stimulus than a more *uniform* response to all anger-provoking stimuli, with the distinctive mark of augmented self-awareness. While this cannot be called a comprehensive common denominator of anger response, it is a permeating psychological trait.

Wolf (6), in one of his publications, stated, in a similar vein, that anger response as an emotion "should be viewed as constituting an essential part of the neural integrative process . . ."; "it may be looked upon as a manifestation or part of reaction pattern aroused as a consequence of the interpretation of life experience. . . ." The concept, "interpretation of life experience," obviously includes Eccles' concept of self-awareness.

We previously set forth the significant contribution of Frank (10) which in substance states that conscious recall affects the effect of a stimulus as to whether it will arouse, modify, augment, or perhaps again suppress an anger response. This is connected with the problem in which way and to what extent learning, memory, and conditioning influences the anger response.

The main difficulty, as it appeared to Rapaport (158), is that there is a "considerably greater amount" of physiological information available about emotions and very little is known about learning and memory. From a merely psychological vantage point, Rapaport has not found that there is necessarily a relationship between memory (learning) and emotions, but "it is possible that the basic psychological factors or dynamics underlying the experience of emotions are identical with those which come to expression in the form of memory organization attributed to emotional influence."

Rapaport enumerates the various psychological approaches to the theory of memory and learning, none of which is satisfactory. Even the technical terms applied in outlining the various theories are vague and ambiguous. "Active process of reconstruction in which selective forces appear".... "the selective forces may be considered representatives of the emotional influence on memory"..., "memory has emerged from the primitive instinctual response and developed through the level of 'habit.'" It hardly must be evidenced that terms such as "reconstruction," "selective forces," level of 'habit,'" and others have little or no meaning, either logically or psychologically or, above all, physiologically. They are all expedient evasions of the essentials. Rapaport deserves credit that he only reports and does not take any position, but he is in error in that the physiological approach to memory * (and learning) has not been extensively investigated, as will be set forth presently when we embark on "informative communication."

In a previous chapter, we enumerated stimuli which may cause an anger response. We shall try to evaluate these stimuli

---

*Recently, J. Olds et al (California Institute of Technology), in mapping 400 points of rat brains with the computer, provisionally identified four areas responsible for memory storage: ventral reticular formation, posterior thalamus, neocortex, and hippocampus. We have omitted the controversial animal experiments by E. R. John, D. Wittons, Willows H. Hyden, G. Ungar, and others.

physiologically, inasmuch as physiological knowledge permits us to do so. What we have called and interpreted as "informative communication" elsewhere (37) is the most frequent stimulus prompting an anger response. We may reiterate that "information" comprises signals or messages originating in a field: These stimuli are, as regards the anger response, selective and transitory, but may be conditioned to become repetitive communication; they are a relation between persons who select signals and messages. Informative communication, then, is a "transmission of messages or signals" by means of exclamations, words, sentences, situations, actions, and also by means of recollection of previously transmitted messages or signals which are in a direct or indirect way associated with present circumstances.

The theory of memory, psychologically and physiologically, will not be scruntinized here profoundly, but an interesting hypothesis has been reported on recall via reverberating neuronal circuits. Also, experiments supporting "a consolidation hypothesis" suggest that a reverberating mechanism may account for some "temporary retention prior to permanent storage" (159, 160). In contrast to informative communication – as a stimulus causing a laughing reaction (37), one engendering an anger response may or may not be meaningful. Thus, the transmitted information may be intelligible and consistent, or it may be misunderstood, misinterpreted. or even nonsensical (e.g. an invective out of context with the situation).

Since McCulloch (161) and his collaborators have set forth the well-corroborated hypothesis that information from the outside (optic and acoustic mainly in the case of anger) is fed in and elaborated in reverberating circuits of neurons at various brain levels and are formed here into "meaning and memory," we can accept von Bonin's (162) statement that "the formal laws of cortical events should be translatable into formal laws of psychological events."

The generally accepted "mechanism of emotion," as indicated by Papez (163), adapted later to the theory of reverberating neuronal circuits, outlined a circuit starting from the hypothalamus via the mammillothalamic bundle to the anterior nucleus of the thalamus, thence to the cingulate gyrus or limbic sector, then to the cornu ammonis, and, from there, by way of the fimbria and the fornix back to the mammillary bodies. This is an elaborate reverberating circuit in which impulses can be conveyed over short or long periods of time. Furthermore, the hypothalamus has direct neuronal connections with the frontal lobes and also is the trigger point of the "mechanism of emotions."

The "relay" circuits which connect the hypothalamus and the frontal lobes have been demonstrated by Spiegel (164), using the pathway of the septal nuclei and medial forebrain bundle to reach the dorsomedial thalamic nuclei and the periventricular system. Some experiments have manifested that electrical stimulation of Brodman's area 24 (medial side of the brain in the anterior part of the gyrus cinguli) effects sympathetic discharges such as pupillary dilatation and rise in blood pressure.

Tinley and Riley (165) have pointed out that from the medial nucleus (auditory impulses) and the lateral geniculate ganglion (visual impulses), internuncial neurons carry the "relatively simple" impulses to the dorsomedial nucleus of the thalamus and, from there, to the hypothalamus, "where they are integrated and projected to the frontal cortex". . . . "All sensation is integrated to form a general background of pleasantness or unpleasantness for the activity of the frontal cortex," and Gillilan (166) adds that this "provides" the feeling tone "for the particular reaction of the individual to any situation." Ruch (167), in a similar fashion, has called attention to the fact that "quite possibly Papez's system serves . . . subjective aspects of emotion. There is, in fact, some evidence that the hippocampal formation is concerned with the subjective or inner aspect of emotion."

From the hypothalamus (especially the posterior and lateral region in which electric stimulation causes extensive sympathetic discharges, producing dilatation of the pupils, elevation of blood pressure, and acceleration of the heart beat), the fibers of the sympathetic division join in the midbrain, pass through the pons and medulla oblongata, and terminate in the spinal cord, where they connect with the peripheral sympathetic ganglia. The sympathetic fibers of the cervical ganglion chain seperate from the main sympathetic route in the upper part of the medulla oblongata and course in a special pathway in the lateral part. The fibers descend in the spinal cord and enter the area of the eighth cervical and first thoracic segments, the inferior cervical or stellate ganglion of the sympathetic chain that supplies head and neck by way of the inferior, middle, and superior ganglia.

Aside from dilatation of pupils, blood pressure rise, and speeding up of pulse rate, sweating sometimes is a symptom of the anger response. The "emotional sweating" which generally involves hands and feet (168) is rarely observed in anger response. Most often, the sweating is limited to the head region (forehead, temples). According to Gillilan (166), "the sympathetic postganglionic neurons begin in the superior cervical ganglion and distribute in the perivascular plexuses. Terminally, most fibers join the branches of the trigeminal nerve." Yet, there are also sympathetic fibers to sweat glands which join the facial nerve. These sympathetic fibers are essentially responsible for the above mentioned sweating of the head regions and have been found in the auriculotemporal and greater auricular nerves.

In this connection, we may point to a dissimilar feature sometimes observed in anger responses — namely, dryness of the mouth. It is caused by "viscous salivary secretion" which indicates, also, predominance of sympathetic discharges in some human emotional reactions (23).

The increased tonus of some muscles, especially the facial and neck muscles, frequently associated with anger response has not been explained consistently. The motor component of the facial nerve arises in the motor nucleus situated in the lateral tegmental area of the caudal region of the pons; it supplies not only the muscles of facial expression but also the platysma and some auricular muscles such as the stapedius. There are investigators who have supposed that there exists an immediate influence of the sympathetic division of the autonomic nervous system on striated muscles.

Others have contended that a direct firing of sympathetic centers, particularly in the hypothalamus, acts on extrapyramidal neurons. As an example, Gellhorn (23) adduces anoxia, which may occur in electroshock treatment, and in which "sympathetic and somatic reactivity is greatly increased and consequently generalized convulsions take place which are accompanied by sympathetic discharges." In anger response, in which short stopping of inspiration and expiration may occur, meaning a brief period of hypoxia, the hypothalamic sympathetic discharges exceed the somatic nerve reactions.

As regards a very enlightening discussion of the problem of muscular tonus, we refer to Schilder (170), who has investigated muscular tonus as a psychosomatic phenomenon. "... We can thus see how every state of mind is in connection with a special state of muscle tonus." "We can, therefore, say that very likely every impression causes a reaction in a tonic way. . . . "Very likely in tonic reactions we deal with an action which is in connection with a very primitive type of perception and with changes of consciousness and the vasovegetative system." All of this does not explain completely the mostly limited, increased muscular tonus in anger reactions, but it affords a direction of further investigation.

Both vasodilatation and vasoconstriction of the face vessels may be observed in anger response. Gillilan (166) states that although the sympathetic division of autonomic nervous system produces peripheral vasoconstriction, peripheral vasodilatation also occurs, "and many times it is a very rapid phenomenon. . . . It may accompany emotional states in which the area affected is usually limited to the face and the hands." Gellhorn (23) points out that both the sympathetic and the parasympathetic divisions of the autonomic nervous system may, at times, be activated in emotional reactions. "... The problem of the relation between emotion and autonomic discharge is complicated by the fact that different persons may react differently in situations presumably eliciting the same kind of emotional disturbance. Gellhorn quotes Richter (171). who reported that during the air attacks on London, some individuals showed pallor of the face; others, flushing of the face. Gellhorn's statement that at times both divisions of the autonomic nervous system can become operative in emotional reactions is a post facto observation, not a causal explantation. Yet, the above recorded fact of peripheral vasodilalation in emotional reactions, which show sympathetic representation prevailingly, evidences that cholinergic sympathetic fibers can generate a paradoxical vasomotor effect which generally is found in emotional states with parasympathetic representation.

Lacrimation is a very infrequent accompaniment of anger response, yet it occurs, particularly in females. Lacrimation in anger response is reflex lacrimation, which is conducted by way of the sensory fibers of the fifth cranial nerve. "From the sensory nuclei of the fifth cranial nerve in the pons and medulla oblongata, internuclear connections complete the arc of the lachrymal nucleus of the seventh nerve" (23). The lacrimal glands receive sympathetic innervation through "a synapse in the superior cervical ganglion and over the carotid plexus" (23). The terminal course of the postganglionic sympathetic fibers is in conjuction with the ophthalmic nerve yet some sympathetic fibers may accompany the zygomatic nerve. The parasympathetic fibers also participate in reflex lacrimation, as has been indicated in a previous publication (37). In spite of the fact that in some rare symptoms the parasympathetic division may play some part in the anger response, this emotional response is essentially sympathetic in somatic representation.

We have noted that hypoglycemia may have a stimulating effect to an anger response. It is well known, as already briefly alluded to, that hypoglycemia is associated with increased secretion of epinephrine and adrenal-cortical steroids (172), which is due to the activity of the sympathetic division of the autonomic nervous system. In fact, it is generally recognized that epinephrine, or preferably norepinephrine, is the "neural transmitter" for the sympathetic nervous system, as it is directly secreted into the blood by the adrenal medulla due to sympathetic central discharges. It also has been established that norepinephrine plays an important role in sympathetic activation in the metabolic field (6). Thus, hypoglycemic anger responses are physiologically explainable by increased sympathetic activity, represented by hypersecretion of epinephrine and norepinephrine as well as cortical steroids.

We have started out this chapter on evaluation with a principal phenomenon of anger response, a phenomenon which becomes particularly manifest after the external stimulus we call "informative communication" — denoting the person-to-person relationship characterized by conveyance of an "adequate" (or inadequate) message or signal from one person to the apperceptive mechanism (sensory perception plus elaboration by reverberating cerebral circuits) of another person.

We have already enumerated several possibilities which may be responsible for, or contribute to, this peculiar sensation of relatively localized discomfort. We will revert to this phenomenon again, because it is so characteristic of the anger response. It has been recognized by a number of authors, but there is no unanimity of opinions.

McLean (173) assumed that the integration required for crude awareness may be completed by the diencephalon, but "that which is required for emotional experience cannot be completed at this level." The appreciation of "various qualities of experience and their association such as ... anger ... undoubtedly requires integration in the cerebral cortex." There is some indirect experimental evidence for this assumption. It has been reported, for instance, that electric stimulation of an area anterior to the premotor cortical region effects bilateral pupillary dilatation, which is abolished by cervical sympathectomy. Such experiments are corroborative evidence that the sympathetic autonomic nervous system is represented in the frontal cerebral cortex. This is obviously important when one considers the psychosomatic perspective of the anger response. Stimulation of the posterior part of the hypothalamus initiates a sympathetic discharge which, among other reactions (elevation of blood pressure and acceleration of heart beat), produces dilatation of the pupils in the same fashion as electrical stimulation of a certain area of the frontal cortex. The described symptoms are — physiologically — part and parcel of the anger response.

Before the "emotional mechanism" as described by Papez (163) was adapted to the concept of reverberating neuronal circuits, Papez was of the opinion that emotional experience was initiated by the hippocampal formation and was integrated in the cerebral cortex, particularly in the cingulate gyrus, which he regarded as "the receptive region for emotional experience." In a negative way, Kuntz (21) set forth that even if our knowledge of visceral (i.e. autonomic) reactions were complete in every detail, it still would not give us a scientific account of the "emotional awareness,"since it does not explain the fact "that the individual knows that he is angry." This is an indirect inference that cortical activity is necessary to bring about the awareness of the anger response.

Although, as already indicated, hypothalamic-cortical connections are known to exist, and although the apperceptive reverberating circuits of the frontal cerebral area (on several levels) as hypothesized by McCulloch and associates may become functionally integrated with Papez' well-established reverberating circuit, thus possibly explicating a dynamic integration of the hypothalamic and frontal area functions, the specific sensation of discomfort, tension, and pressure in the upper thoracic region in the anger response is not satisfactorily explained.

For the time being, we must content ourselves with Montagu's (24) already quoted observation that awareness of the activity of the sympathetic nervous system is characterized by sensations of discomfort and unpleasantness. When we combine the just-adduced hypotheses and observations with the above-indicated data as reported by Gillilan and Wolf and Wolff, we may gain some understanding of the physiological determinants which may underlie the peculiar intrathoracic experience to a stimulus of "informative communication," even when we are not yet able to comprehend this sensation as a singular, specific reaction.

An exteroceptive stimulus, which we have touched upon, to produce an anger response is noise. We have determined above the definition of noise. Auditory radiation fibers from the medial geniculate ganglion terminate in the temporal lobe. It has been found experimentally that stimulation of the superior temporal gyrus in man — posterior to the fissure Rolandi, close to the Sylvian fissure, and also in the depth of this fissure — produce buzzing, clicking, and rumbling sounds, i. e. noise (174, 175). The nucleus of the lateral leminiscus has fiber connections with the reticular formation from where they course to various motor nuclei and to the inferior colliculus; here is the auditory reflex center, which is connected with the spinal accessory nucleus and the motor cells of the spinal cord by way of the reticulobulbar and reticulospinal tracts. These tracts are derived from reticular nuclei in the upper medulla oblongata (176).

Although no connections with the sympathetic nervous system are expressly indicated, the sites of the auditory pathways would afford some possibilities for such connections. It may be of interest that a noise experiment in decorticated cats has rendered such a connection likely. "The moment the noise was heard, the cat abruptly retracted and lowered its head, crouched, mewed, and then dashed off, running rapidly in a slinking manner, with head, chest, belly and tail close to the floor. After blindly colliding with several objects in her path, she came to rest in a corner, where she crouched mewing plaintively, with eyes and pupils wide and the hair of back and tail erected." Bard (177), who described this experiment has called it an anger response. It goes without saying that all depicted signs are due to sympathetic discharges upon noise stimulation in a decorticated animal. The signs and symptoms are quite different from sham rage. Gellhorn (23) also confirms that the autonomic discharge in this animal is predominantly sympathetic.

If we venture to draw a generalized conclusion from this one experiment, we may assume that in the anger response to a noise stimulus, sympathetic discharges are operative, coming particularly to the fore when the subcortical-cortical connections are interrupted. In this connection, we may call attention to the concept of "shock decortication" and similar terms, denoting the functional abolition of cortical control.

Fatigue, as it was noticed, is a condition which may dispose to anger response. "Fatigue" is difficult to determine as a general phenomenon. Much has been published about muscular fatigue, neuromuscular fatigue, and "cortical" fatigue, but "the restricted meaning of fatigue is not to be confused with the subjective experience encountered by man irrespective of effort and exercise. The experience is a complex response to a variety of conditions, which are an emotional state, difficult breathing, insufficient cardiovascular adjustment, and perhaps even some components of mechanical fatigue" (178). The reasons why "fatigue" may be a physiological basis for anger response to adequate stimuli are not quite clear. It is known that in adrenal insufficiency, stress lowers the resistance level. It is, however, theoretically possible that considerable sympathetic stimulation in this condition may, for a short period of time, increase the output of adrenal or adequate pituitary hormones, thus reversing the state of lowered resistance to one of increased resistance, laying the groundwork for a short-lived anger response. This, however, is highly hypothetical.

Another hypothesis is that hypoglycemia often accompanies adrenal insufficiency and may initiate increased secretion of epinephrine or norepinephrine and cortical steroids; this may be another theoretical possibility as to why fatigue, in a specific situation, may become interrupted by an anger response. Adrenal insufficiency is only an isolated instance of fatigue as a symptom, and this example would not suffice for generalizations. It does, however, serve as a model that in specific cases, the symptom of fatigue can be disrupted by sympathetic discharges and, therefore, could be represented psychologically as anger responses if appropriate stimuli are operative.

We already have pointed out that hunger may facilitate anger responses. The afferent pathway of visceral sensations is obviously parasympathetic. Afferent vagal impulses which convey hunger sensation terminate in the orbital cortex of the frontal lobes (179), while changes in the water metabolism of the tissues stimulate the supraoptic nuclei of the hypothalamus (180) and, by way of the central thalamic nuclei, reach the cortex (181) — whereas in animals experiments, lesions and destruction of the ventromedial nucleus of the hypothalamus show that the downward discharge may be, at least in part, conveyed by sympathetic pathways.

In man, the caudal region of the hypothalamus, which is a sympathetic center, is not clearly limited, so that there is some overlapping area of sympathetic and parasympathetic centers. The posterior and lateral nuclei of the hypothalamus are essentially responsible for the sympathetic outflow, but there is not a quite rigid border from the ventromedial nucleus, and neurons may transgress the nuclear lines (23). Hetherington and Ranson (182) showed, in animal experiments, that not only the ventromedial but also the dorsomedial nuclei in the rat are involved in hyperphagia (hunger?). From a clinical point of view, Nasset has pointed out that hunger contractions of the stomach are associated with hyperexcitability of the central nervous system;

objective signs of this association can be elicited. A manifestation which occurs in hunger periods is, among others, increase in pulse rate, which is obviously due to sympathetic stimulation (183). Whether this is an acceptable hypothesis remains to be investigated.

Touch was previously mentioned as a stimulus which may prompt an anger response — but not the tactile perception proper, but touch only as a "gesture" which carries a special meaning, an "informative communication," such as condescendence, didacticism, arrogance, fraternalization, admonition, criticism, amusement.

In spite of the fact that the tactile stimulus engenders an anger response only when it carries an "informative communication," it may be in order to pursue the touch sensation from its cutaneous perception to the central nervous system. Cutaneous tactile sensibility originates in various sensory receptors such as Merkel's tactile corpuscle, Meissner's tactile corpuscle, and the reticular net surrounding the hair follicle.

The touch sensation has its afferent pathway in the ventral spinothalamic tract which arises in cells of the dorsal gray column at the opposite side of the spinal cord. The ventral spinothalamic tract enters the lateral nucleus of the thalamus. From there is a fiber connection with the parietal lobe of the brain, particularly the cortical areas 3-1-2 of the somesthetic cortex which is considered the central cortical region for the touch sensation.

While all cortical touch representations of cutaneous areas are contralateral, the skin of the face is represented bilaterally in the cortex. The thalamus also has, as previously evidenced, connections with the hypothalamus, the sympathetic outflow of which is situated particularly in the posterior and lateral region. Because of this thalamo-cortical and thalamo-hypothalamic interrelationship, there is a hypothetical possibility that the central touch apperception becomes involved in the various cortical reverberating circuits as well as in the circuit of Papez, so that the touch apperception may become an "informative" stimulus. Thus, an anger response may result from this type of touch sensation.

In contrast to the touch stimulus, a simple light stimulus, as previously described, which generally does not result in an optic image, may provoke an anger response. It was Gellhorn (23) who stressed that "if the intensity and duration of (light) stimualtion are sufficient, sympathetic excitation leads to adrenomedullary secretion." Thus, a sudden and unexpected exposure to a light stimulus, which produces an anger response, it physiologically represented by a sympathetically prompted increase in adrenal-medullary secretion, which is most frequently found in anger response.

5

COMMENT

THE anger response is one of those "minor" psychosomatic phenomena which — though an everyday experience of almost everyone — has not been investigated in detail as yet, either psychologically, physiologically, or as to the pathological conditions in which anger response is a factor. More than any other emotional reaction, it has been taken for granted and has been thrown together with other unpleasant emotional reactions without determining the well-established delimitation and consistent differentiation from other, ostensibly similar, emotional reactions. This delimitation is interesting and significant.

In a previous chapter we have tried to show that anger response is a singular, well-defined emotional response, not only in psychological respect but, in a more relative way, from a physiological point of view, because anger responses in most of their signs and symptoms correspond with stimulation of the sympathetic division of the autonomic nervous system. It could also be shown that anger responses, essentially because of this physiological representation, can be manifested in a number of pathological syndromes.

It became evident that the stimuli which produce anger responses are limited not only in number but also as to specificity. Another important observation is that these stimuli in different situations and under different conditions could cause emotional reactions which differ from anger responses. For instance, a given stimulus may prompt in one person a considerable acceleration of the pulse rate (sympathetic stimulation) and in another individual a slowing of the pulse rate (parasympathetic stimulation). The same holds true for the identical person when the stimulus is experienced in different situations or environmental conditions.

We also are aware of the fact that stimuli which induce

emotional reactions and, ~~therewith~~, specific "downward" autonomic discharges may be distinguished or modified by inherent individual traits (e.g. sympatheticotonic constitutional types, amphotic constitutional types, etc., according to Sheldon — references 131, 132). It also should be kept in mind that in infrequent circumstances, parasympathetic effects may be obtained by stimulation of the posterior hypothalamus with low frequency currents, although with higher frequency stimulation, the parasympathetic discharges are at once replaced by sympathetic effects (184). We already have touched upon the occasional overlapping of sympathetic and parasympathetic activity. Thus, in some instances, at the beginning of an emotional response, parasympathetic "downward" effects may be recognizable, which, however, with increasing intensity of the stimulus are replaced by sympathetic effects. This physiological situation may explain the frequent confusion of anger responses with emotional reactions differing not only psychologically but also in their physiological representation.

As one example, it may be instructive to consider hostility. This word is derived from the Latin "hostis," which means enemy. Enmity is open antagonism against one or many individuals. There may be also a hostility against ideas, dogmas, but only when they are represented by persons. Hostility is generally a long-lasting affective phenomenon, which may persist, once established, without repeated stimuli. This is one essential difference from anger response. Another is that hostility is always directed against a person or persons, either the person as an individual or as a representative or agent of an ideology or action-complex.

Hostility is not directed against a material object (with exception that it serves as doctrinal symbol) and also not against oneself. One can be angry with a non-functioning object and with oneself in the sense of frustration. It has been argued in the psychoanalytical literature that hostility against oneself is possible and that self-destruction tendencies and suicide attempts exemplify this (185). Without entering into a detailed discussion, it appears that in self-destructive and suicidal ideas and acts there is simply a surrender, abdication, of the drive to self-preservation and a loss or deprivation of identity. This is a process, which is in our judgment, quite different from hostility. Hostility is a positive, dynamic emotional reaction directed against the stimulus. Self-destruction and suicide are negative, self-derogating, self-disparaging, identity-denying behavior impairmants, not directed against a stimulus which produces hostility.

This, in our opinion, erroneous concept of hostility against oneself is probably derived from the old psychiatric experience that depressed patients may exhibit hostility. "In depression ego-alien impulses, i.e. hostile impulses, can no longer be excluded from consciousness by repression." It is questionable whether "ego-alien impulses" (this in itself is a "contradictio in adjecto," as all impulses originate in the ego, while drives, which are not reactive, arise in the id) are, indeed, "hostile" impulses. First of all, hostility is a reaction and not an impulse (from Latin "impellere" — to urge), and secondly, no ego "alien" reactions could be hostile, because the very characteristic of hostility is ego involvement and not ego alienation.

When we consider hostility and anger in the perspective of Selye's general adaptation syndrome (49), we may assume that both are alarm reactions evoked by certain stressors. This parallel cannot be maintained beyond the alarm reaction. In hostility, a state of resistance can be maintained as long as hostility is repressed and remains subconscious, or as long as conscious hostility is not exacerbated by new, adequate, and/or repeated stimuli. These may cause an "adaptational crisis" and thus may lead to the last stage of the general adaptation syndrome, the state of exhaustion. In this state, resistance is no longer sustained and, although some of the alarm reaction hostile attitudes may sporadically recur, the exhaustion state is distinguished by a cessation of active emotional reactions, by a withdrawal from reality, and/or by regression to paranoid attitudes. In anger, on the other hand, after a short alarm reaction, the state of resistance or adaptation will never break down by the appearance of an adaptational crisis," as the single episode of an anger response is generally short-lived, so that a state of exhaustion will not occur. The organism will reattain homeostasis.

Another quite apparent difference between anger response and hostility is that the latter is by far not as clearly delimited as is the former one. Hostility can easily transmute or enhance into aggression, which is distinguished by motor expression. Freud (185) has even linked hostility and aggression together, as both may be expected to be directed "toward those factors interfering with the pleasure principle."

Dunbar (186) stated that aggression would be expected "to be characterized by a tendency to attack others directly or symbolically. It may be directed outwardly against the world or become manifest in internalized conflicts as observed in some psychosomatic disorders." Aside from the already mentioned fact that hostility is generally an enduring, expanding, and overshooting emotional reaction in contradistinction to the anger response which is limited as to time, intensity, and symptomatology, hostility may also prompt neurotic phenomena at times in form of conversion reactions or psychosomatic signs and symptoms. This does not occur in anger responses.

There is no doubt that in hostility and aggression, sympathetic discharges are operative as they are in anger responses. In contrast to anger responses, where parasympathetic effects are only either rare or temporary, they are by far more prevalent than sympathetic activity in hostility and aggression. Gellhorn (23) has even emphasized that hostility causes predominantly parasympathetic discharges. Holmes and associates (187) have pointed out that motor activity and vascularity are increased not only under conditions of "pleasurable thoughts of eating" but also in situations prompting "aggressive feelings including . . . hostility." These are parasympathetic reactions to stimuli.

Gellhorn (23), in his book, stressed a shifting autonomic effect in aggression. In one instance aggression may be accompanied by a sympathetic downward discharge with accelerated heart rate, increased cardiac output, and peripheral vascular resistance followed by blood pressure elevation. In other instances, or even in the same individual at different times, a depressor response may be found if hostility is associated with depression; the cold pressure test results in a fall in blood pressure, which means that the generally anticipated sympathetic effect has shifted to a parasympathetic effect.

While depression is not an underlying condition in anger

responses, the importance of hostility as a feature of depression has also been emphasized by Whitehorn (188): "Psychopathologically depressed patients exhibit stiff-necked resistance; one senses in many bitterness and hatefulness. The perception of this component of hostility ... is a point of disagreement among psychiatrists. Some assume an element of hostility in all depressive psychotics as part of the mechanism; others admit its presence only on overwhelming testimony; still others perceive evidence of hostile feeling in many depressed patients without assuming its universality in depressions."

We believe that we have adduced a considerable number of relevant facts which support our contention that the anger response must be differentiated and separated physiologically and psychologically from allegedly cognate emotional reactions such as hostility and aggression.

It may be instructive, in this connection, to revert briefly to the electroencephalographic peculiarities which have been reported in anger responses as set forth in the second chapter. We have found that several electroencephalographers have distinctly demonstrated short runs of delta (theta) activity or spikes during anger response, or at least a slowing down of the alpha pattern. It is significant that random slow activity with disappearance of alpha waves follows intravenous injection of epinephrine, which seems to prove that the similar electrographic pattern in anger response is associated with sympathetic stimulation (189).

There is also a report stating that in hypoglycemia, which at times has found to be associated with anger response, and which is known to induce increased secretion of epinephrine and norepinephrine, alpha activity is gradually diminished and bursts of delta activity are observed (190). These observations have been confirmed by Brazier and associates (191) and by Strauss and Wechsler (192).

That delta wave activity orginates in the region of the hypothalamus has been pointed but by H. Strauss (74) on various occasions. The same author has stated that "apprehensiveness and emotional stress" usually depress the amount of alpha activity, which is replaced by "low voltage random frequency activity." Strauss avoids the term "anger," but he emphasizes that "the provocation of delta waves by anxiety-laden situations is *not* generally accepted today." This apparently can be interpreted that in depression (in which considerable anxiety is often a factor), delta activity is not characteristic as it is in anger response.

Strauss has also touched upon the "startle" response, which is a rare but possible initial component of the anger response, and he asserted that a startle response, "no matter how provoked," is always associated with depression of alpha wave activity. Brazier and collaborators (193) have evidenced that in anxiety neurosis, a rather rapid activity of the beta type is common, differing from the normal alpha band and the delta (theta) wave pattern during an anger response.

No electroencephalographic investigations could be detected in the literature in association with hostility. There are many reports about electroencephalographic findings in aggressive behavior, but they do not refer to aggressive tendencies in the course of hostility. Most reports deal with overt aggression, and aggression associated with alcoholism, and/or addiciton; in some instances, aggressiveness resembled electroencephalographically the dysrhythmic pattern found in the "larval epileptic phenomenon," which occasionally has been encountered in aggressive psychopaths. Hill (194) is of the opinion that these dysrythmias are related to a developmental disorder of tha basal gray ganglia. At any rate, the dysrhytmic electroencephalographic pattern of aggression is clearly dissimilar from the delta (theta) wave burst pattern of anger responses and serves as more evidence that aggressive tendencies are not components of the anger response.

We have set out to consider another of the "minor" problems of the human organism. From a statistical point of view, the anger response, taking into account the general population, is a unique example of a 100 percent incidence rate, a 100 percent period prevalence rate, with a probability ratio of close to one. This statistical phenomenon simply indicates that anger response is an emotional observational fact which occurs and will occur in every individual, unless he is severely physically and mentally disabled, as a universal experience.

Our main goal has been to establish the anger response as a psychosomatic entity, one which can be delimited psychologically, consistently determined physiologically, and which — according to its characteristic properties and functions — may correlatively appear as a symptom in a number of medical impairments.

As every human being — unless he is completely incapacitated by congenital or acquired damage of the central nervous and/or endocrine systems — has the potential to experience anger response, the problem of heredity arises. In all probability, the genetic character is autosomal dominant, the phenotype must be blue-printed by multiple genes, the penetrance appears to be complete, while the expressivity seems to be somewhat variable. In a recent paper, Benzer (195) stresses that the genes determine "anatomical and biochemical features." What Benzer obviously refers to is that the genes, as Montagu (196) has expressed it, are "most usefully looked upon as chemical packages of potentialities." In this vein, Benzer continues "It should not be surprising if, to a large degree, the genes also determine behavioral temperament, although [according to Hirsch (197) and many others] environmental influences can also play a large role."

"All behavior is inevitably the resultant of both components." This is certainly true in considering the hereditary involvement in the anger response. As Benzer again has well stated "To discern the genetic contribution clearly, the thing to do is to keep the environment constant and change the genes. This is not easy to do with human beings..., particularly if one must wait generations for the result." As to anger response, we may be justified to add that environmental stimuli are a nesessity, and that the phenotype of anger is under all circumstances the effect of a genetic "potentiality" and an environmental specificity.

Weiss (198) has wisely stated "The primary aim of research must not be just more facts, but more facts of strategic value. I mean that property of an observation or an experiment that leads to the clarification or solution of a problem, or deeper insight into a phenomenon, to the linking of previously unrelated facts and ideas...."

REFERENCES

1. English, A. B., and English, A. C.: *A Comprehensive Dictionary of Psychological and Psychoanalytical Terms.* New York, Longmans, Green, 1958.
2. Eccles, J. C.: *The Neurophysiological Basis of Mind.* Oxford, Clarendon Press, 1953.
3. Whitehead, A. N.: *Symbolism. Its Meaning and Effect.* New York, Macmillan, 1927.
4. Fischer, S.: *Principles of General Psychopathology.* New York, Philosophical Library, 1950.
5. Sullivan, H. Stack.: Quoted in Mullahy, P.: *The Contributions of Harry Stack Sullivan* (Unpublished Material). New York, Hermitage House, 1952.
6. Wolf, S.: Emotions and the autonomic nervous system. *Arch Int Med 126:*1070, 1970.
7. Menninger, K.: *A Psychiatrist's World. The Selected Papers.* New York, Viking Press, 1959.
8. Menninger, K., et al: *The Vital Balance.* New York, Viking Press, 1967 (Martin Luther, *Table Talk,* Vol. CCCXIX, 1569).
9. Kubie, L. S.: Neurotic potential and human adaptation. In von Foerster, H. (Ed.): *Cybernetics.* New York, Josiah Macy Foundation, 1950.
10. Frank, L. K.: In discussion of "Recall and Recognition." In von Foerster, H. (Ed.): *Cybernetics.* New York, Josiah Macy Foundation, 1950.
11. Lehmann, H. E.: Time and psychopathology. In Fischer, K. (Ed.): Interdisciplinary perspectives of time. *Ann Aca Sci, 138:*2, 1967.
12. Brown, J. A. C.: Frustration and aggression. A Study of frustration in relation to army life. *J Soc Psychol, 85:*101, 1945.
13. Cameron, D. E.: *General Psychotherapy.* New York, Grune & Stratton, 1950.
14. Kaplan, D. M., and Goodrich, W.: A formulation for interpersonal anger. *Am J Orthopsychiatry, 27:*387, 1957.
15. Jersild, A. T., et al: *The Meaning of Psychotherapy in the Teacher's Life and Work.* New York, Columbia University Press, 1962.
16. Yacorzynski, G. K.: *Medical Psychology.* New York, Ronald Press, 1951.
17. Abrahamson, D.: *The Road to Emotional Maturity.* Englewood Cliffs,

N. J., Prentice-Hall, 1958.
18. Canfield, N.: *Audiology, The Science of Hearing.* Springfield, Thomas, 1949.
19. Cleghorn, R.: Steroid hormones in relation to neuropsychiatric disorder. In Hoagland, H. (Ed.): *Hormones, Brain Function and Behavior.* New York, Academic Press, 1957.
20. Gibson, J. G.: Emotions and the thyroid gland. *J Psychosom Res, 6:*91, 1962.
21. Kuntz, A.: *Visceral Innervation and Its Relation to Personality.* Springfield, Thomas, 1951.
22. Gates, G. S.: An observational study of anger. *J Exp Psychol, 9:*325, 1926.
23. Gellhorn, E.: *Physiological Foundations of Neurology and Psychiatry.* Minneapolis, University of Minnesota Press, 1953.
24. Montagu, Ashley, M. F.: *The Direction of Human Development. Biological and Social Bases.* New York, Harper & Brothers, 1955.
25. Freud, S.: *Repression. Collected Papers, Volume IV,* London, Hogarth Press.
26. Bachelard, G.: *La dialectique de la durée.* Paris, Bovin, 1936.
27. Fraisse, P.: *The Psychology of Time* (translated by J. Leith). New York, Harper & Row, 1963.
28. Cohn, J.: The concept of goal gradients: A review of its present status. *J Nerv Ment Dis, 49:*303, 1953.
29. Watson, J. B.: *Behaviorism.* New York, Norton Company, 1925.
30. Watson, J. B.: What nursery has to say about instincts. *J Gen Psychol 32:*293, 1925.
31. Goodenaugh, F. L.: *Anger in Young Children.* Minneapolis, University of Minnesota Press, 1931.
32. Hicks, J. A., and Hayes, M.: Study of the characteristics of 250 junior high school children. *Child Develop, 9:*219, 1938.
33. Gates, G. S.: An Observation Study of Anger. *J Exp Psychol, 9:*325, 1926.
34. Meltzer, H.: Students' adjustments in anger. *J Social Psychol, 4:*285, 1933.
35. Anastasia, A., Cohen, W., and Spatz, D. A.: A study of fear and anger in college students through the controlled diary method. *J Gen Psychol, 73:*243, 1948.
36. Gutheil, E. A.: *The Handbook of Dream Analysis.* New York, Liveright Publishing, 1951.
37. Stearns, F. R.: *Laughing. Physiology, Pathophysiology, Psychology, Pathopsychology and Development.* Springfield, Thomas, 1972.
38. Canfield, N.: *Audiology, The Science of Hearing.* Springfield, Thomas 1949.
39. McLord, C. P., et al: Noise and its effect on human beings. *JAMA, 110:*1553, 1938.

40. Stearns, F. R.: Noise and health. *J Human Ecol, 1:*1, 1952.
41. Saltzman, M.: *Clinical Audiology.* New York, Grune & Stratton, 1949.
42. Peterson, W. F.: *Man – Weather – Sun.* Springfield, Thomas, 1948.
43. Young, P. T.: Laughing and weeping, cheerfulness and depression. A study of moods among college students. *J Soc Psychol, 8:*311, 1937.
44. Stratton, G. M.: Emotion and the Incidence of disease: The influence of the diseases and of the age at which they occur. *Psychol Review, 36:*242, 1929.
45. Selye, H.: *The Physiology and Pathology of Exposure to Stress,* Montreal, Acta, Inc., 1950.
46. Selye, H.: *The Stress of Life.* New York, McGraw-Hill, 1956.
47. Wolf, S., and Wolff, H. G.: The gastric mucosa, "Gastritis and Ulcer." *Am J Digest Dis, 10:*23, 1943.
48. Wolf, S., and Wolff, H. G.: Life situations, emotions and gastric function: A Summary. In Weider, A., and Wechsler, D. (Eds.): *Contributions Toward Medical Psychology.* New York, Ronald Press, 1953, Vol. I, ch. 13.
49. Wolf, S.: Emotions and the automomic nervous system. *Arch Intern Med, 126:*1024, 1970.
50. Abrahams, V. C., and Hilton, S. M.: Active muscle vasodilatation and its relation to the "Flight and Fright Reactions in the Conscious Animal." *J Physiol, 140:*161, 1957.
51. Bard, P.: Control of systemic blood vessels. In Bard, P. (Ed.): *Medical Physiology,* 11th ed. St. Louis, C. V. Mosby 1961, ch. 11.
52. Wolf, S.: *The Stomach.* New York, Oxford University Press, 1965.
53. Beaumont, W.: *Experiments and Observations on the Gastric Juice and The Physiology of Digestion.* Pittsburg, F. P. Allen, 1833.
54. Hornborg, A. F.: Beiträge zur Kenntniss der Absonderungsbedingungen des Magensaftes beim Menschen. *Skandinav Arch Physiol, 15:*209, 1904.
55. Bogen, H.: Experimentelle Untersuchungen über psychische und assoziative Magensekretion beim Menschen. *Arch Physiol, 117:*150, 1907.
56. Schrottenbach, H.: Studien über den Einfluss der Grosshirntätigkeit auf die Magensekretion des Menschen. *Ztschr Neurol Psychiat, 69:*254, 1921.
57. McGregor, H. G.: *Emotional Factor in Visceral Disease,* London, Oxford University Press, 1938.
58. Mittelmann, B., and Wolff, H. G.: Emotions and gastrointestional functions: Experimental studies with gastritis, duodenitis and peptic ulcer. *Psychosom Med, 4:*5, 1942.
59. Ivy, A. C. Grossman, M. I., and Bachrach, W. H.: *Peptic Ulcer.* Philadelphia, Blakiston, 1950.
60. Smirk, F. H.: Pathogenesis of essential hypertension. *Br Med J* 1949, p. 191.
61. Graham, B. F., Goodman, A. J., Malmo, R. B., Shagass, C., and

Cleghorn, R. A.: Influence of stress on the lymphocyte count in human subjects. *Rev Canad Biol, 7:*183, 1948.
62. Shands, H. G., and Finesinger, J. E.: Lymphocytes in the psychoneuroses. Preliminary observations *Am J Psychiatr, 105:*277, 1948.
63. Hills, A. G., Forsham, P. H., and Finch, C. A.: Changes in circulating leucocytes induced by the administration of pituitary adenocorticotrophic hormone (ACTH) in man. *Blood, 3:*755, 1948.
64. Cardon, P. V., Jr., and Miller, P. S.: *Ann N Y Acad Sci, 125:*924, 1966.
65. Freud, J. M. Manus, B. C., and Mühlbock, O.: Enlarged adrenals after administration of fatty acid extracts of testicles. *Acta Brev Neerland, 8:*6, 1938.
66. Heath, R. C., and Founds, W. L.: A perfusion canula for introcerebral microinjections. *Electroencephalogr Clin Neurophysiol, 12:*930, 1960.
67. Heath, R. C.: Brain centers and control of behavior – man. In Nodine, J. H., and Moyer, J. M. (Eds.): *Psychosomatic Medicine. The First Hahnemann Symposium.* Philadelphia, Lea & Febiger, 1962.
68. Walker, W. G.: *The Living Brain.* New York, W. W. Norton, 1953.
69. Brazier, M. A. B.: *The Electrical Activity of the Nervous System.* London, Pitman, 1951.
70. Gibbs, F. A., and Gibbs, E. U.: *Atlas of Electroencephalography.* Cambridge, Mass., Addison-Wesley, 1950.
71. Metcalf, D. R.: On the development of 6 and 14 per second spikes. *Electroencephalogr Clin Neurophysiol, 11:*616, 1959.
72. Metcalf, D. R.: *Behavioral and Physiological Implication in 6 and 14 per second Spikes and the EEG.* Milwaukee, Proceedings of the Eleventh Symposium, Western Institute in Epilepsy, 1959.
73. Metcalf, D. R.: Controlled studies of the incidence and significance of 6 and 14 per second positive spiking. *Electroencephalogr Clin Neurophysiol, 15:*161, 1963.
74. Strauss, H., et al: *Diagnostic Electroencephalography.* New York, Grune & Stratton, 1952.
75. Delay, J.: *Les ondes cérébrales et la psychologie.* Paris, Presses Universitaires de France, 1942.
76. Oberman, C. H.: The effect on the Berger rhythm of mild affective states. *J Abnorm Social Psychol, 34:*84, 1939.
77. Wilson, W. P. (Ed.): *Applications of Electroencephalography in Psychiatry. A symposium.* Durham, N. C., Duke University Press, 1965.
78. Penfield, W., and Jasper, H.: *Epilepsy and Functional Anatomy of the Human Brain.* Boston, Little, Brown, 1954.
79. Walter, W. G.: Quoted in Schwab, R. S.: *Electroencephalography in Clinical Practice.* Philadelphia, W. B. Saunders, 1951.
80. Kinsey, A. C., et al: *Sexual Behavior in the Human Female.* Philadelphia, W. B. Saunders, 1953.
81. Friedman, A. P.: *Research and Clinical Studies in Headache.* Baltimore, Williams & Wilkins, 1967.

82. Rylander, G.: Mental changes after excision of cerebral tissue. *Acta Neurol Psychiatr (suppl 23, Copenhagen),* 1943.
83. Freeman, W., and Watts, J. W.: *Psychosurgery in the Treatment of Mental Disorders and Intractable Pain.* Springfield, Thomas, 1950.
84. Tow, P. McDonald: *Personality Changes Following Frontal Leukotomy.* London, Oxford University Press, 1955.
85. Porteus, S. D.: Medical applications of the maze test. *Med J Australia, 1:*558, 1944.
86. Porteus, S. D., and Peters, H.: Psychosurgery and test validity. *J Abnorm Soc Psychol, 42:* 493, 1947.
87. Porteus, S. D., and Kepner, R. De M.: Mental changes after bilateral prefrontal lobotomy. *Gen Psychol Monogr, 29:*4-115, 1944.
88. Henrichs, T. F. Mackenzie, J. W., and Almond, C. H.: Psychological adjustment and psychiatric complications following open heart surgery. *J Nerv Ment Dis, 152:*332, 1971.
89. Wolf, S.: Stress and Heart Disease. *Mod Concepts Cardio-Vasc Dis. 29:*599, 1960.
90. McGavack, T. H.: *The Thyroid.* St. Louis, C. V. Mosby, 1951.
91. Zondek, H., and Wolfsohn, G.: Myxedema and psychosis, *Lancet, 2:*438, 1944.
92. Thorn, G. W., and Forsham, P. H.: Part II. Adrenal cortical insufficiency. In Williams, R. H. (Ed.): *Textbook of Endocrinology.* Philadelphia, W. B. Saunders, 1950.
93. Lewis, R. A., Hoffman, W. C., and Thorn, G. W.: The electroencephalogram in Addison's Disease. *Bull Johns Hopkins Hosp, 70:*335, 1942.
94. Talbot, N. B., Sobel, E. H., McArthur, J. W., and Crawford, J. D.: *Functional Endocrinology from Birth Through Adolescence.* Cambridge, Harvard University Press, 1952.
95. Cannon, W.: *The Wisdom of the Body,* New York, W. W. Norton, 1959.
96. Proetz, A. W.: *Applied Physiology of the Nose.* St. Louis, Annals Publishing company, 1941.
97. Holmes, T., Goodell, W., Wolf, S., and Wolff, H. G.: *The Nose: An Experimental Study of Reaction Within the Nose in Human Subjects During Varying Life Experiences.* Springfield, Thomas, 1950.
98. Wolff, H. G.: Life stress and cardiovascular disorders. *Circulation, 1:*187, 1950.
99. Hack: Quoted by Bosworth, F. H.: *Diseases of the Nose and Throat.* New York, W. Wood, 1897.
100. Hansel, F. K.: *Clinical Allergy.* St. Louis, C. V. Mosby, 1953.
101. Lederer, F. L.: *Diseases of the Ear, Nose and Throat,* 6th ed. Philadelphia, F. A. Davis, 1952.
102. Ashley, R.: In discussion of Williams, H. L.: A concept of allergy as autonomic dysfunction suggested as an improved working hypothesis. *Trans Am Aca Ophthalmol, 55:*123, 1950.
103. Wolff, H. G., et al: Stress, emotions and human sebum: Their relevance

to acne vulgaris. *Trans Assoc Am Phys, 44:*435, 1951.
104. Fluhman, C. F.: *The Management of Menstrual Disorders.* Philadelphia, W. B. Saunders, 1956.
105. Crossen, R. J.: *Diseases of Women,* 10th ed. St. Louis, C. V. Mosby, 1953.
106. Maranon, G.: *The Climacteric (The Critical Age)* (Translated by K. S. Steven, edited by C. Culbertson). St. Louis, C. V. Mosby, 1929.
107. Thorn, G. W., et al: A study of the mechanism of edema associated with menstruation. *Endocrinology, 22:*55, 1938.
108. Thorn, G. W., and Harrop, G. A.: The "sodium retaining effect" of sex hormones. *Science, 86:*40, 1937.
109. Morton, J. H.: Quoted by Crossen, R. J.: *Am J Obst Gynecol, 60:*343, 1950.
110. Greenhill, J. P., and Freed, S. C.: Quoted by Crossen, R. J.: *JAMA, 117:*504, 1941.
111. Schiff, L.: The large intestine. In Sodeman, W. A.: *Pathologic Physiology: Mechanism of Disease.* Philadelphia, W. B. Saunders, 1950.
112. Horner, J. L.: Constipation and Diarrhea. In McByde, C. M. (Ed.): *Signs and Symptoms. Their Clinical Interpretation.* Philadelphia, J. B. Lippincott, 1947.
113. Cannon, W. B.: *Bodily Changes in Pain, Hunger, Fear and Rage,* 2nd ed. New York, Appleton-Century-Crofts, 1929.
114. Grace, W. J., Wolf, S., and Wolff, H. G.: *The Human Colon: Experimental Study Based on Direct Observation of Four Fistulous Subjects.* New York, Paul B. Hoeber, 1951.
115. Wechsler, I. S.: *Textbook of Clinical Neurology,* 8th ed. Philadelphia, W. B. Saunders, 1958.
116. Deitch, B., and Shulkin, M. W.: Management of depression with cancer. In Nodine, J. H., and Moyer, J. H.: *Psychosomatic Medicine,* Philadelphia, Lea & Febiger, 1962, ch. 115.
117. Wolf, S., and Wolff, H. G.: *Human Gastric Function,* 2nd ed. New York, Oxford University Press, 1947.
118. Dufault, P., Crane, A. R., and Feinsilver, O.: *The Diagnosis and Treatment of Pulmonary Tuberculosis.* Philadelphia, Lea & Febiger, 1958.
119. Ranson, S. W.: Regulation of body Temperature. In Association for Research in Nervous and Mental Diseases: *The Hypothalamus and Central Levels of Autonomic Function.* Baltimore, Williams & Wilkins, vol. 20, Ch. II.
120. Ranson, S. W., and Magoun, H. W.: The hypothalamus. *Ergebn Physiol, 41:*56, 1939.
121. Dubois, E. F.: *Fever and Regulation of Body Temperature.* Springfield, Thomas, 1948.
122. Brengelman, G., and Brown, A. C.: Temperature regulation. In Ruch, F. C., and Patton, H. D. (Eds.): *Physiolgy and Biophysics.* Philadelphia, W. B. Saunders, 1965.

References

123. Davies, R. J.: Tuberculosis. In Pullen, R. L. (Ed.): *Pulmonary Diseases.* Philadelphia, Lea & Febiger, 1955, Ch. II.
124. Brown, T. McP., Bush, S. W., and Felts, W. R., Jr.: Rheumatoid arthritis and gout. In Wohl, M. G.: *Long-Term Illness.* Philadelphia, W. B. Saunders, 1959, ch. 6.
125. Hench, P. S., Kendall, E. E., Slocumb, C. H., and Polley, H. F.: The effect of a hormone of the adrenal cortex (17-hydroxy-11-dehydrocorticosterone: Compound E) and of pituitary adrenocorticotropic hormone on rheumatoid arthritis. *Proc Staff Meet Mayo Clin, 24:*277, 1949.
126. Bishop, P. M. F.: *Recent Advances in Endocrinology,* 7th ed. London, J. & A. Churchill, Ltd., 1954.
127. Harris, G. W.: Hypothalamic control of the anterior pituitary gland. *Ciba Found Coll Endocrinal, 4:*106, 1952.
128. Wechsler, I. S.: *A Textbook of Clinical Neurology,* 8th ed. Philadelphia, W. B. Saunders, 1958.
129. Kraepelin, E.: *Lectures on Clinical Psychiatry* (translated from the German), New York, William Wood, 1894.
130. Fisher, C. H., Mohr, J. P., and Adams, R. D.: Cerebrovascular diseases. In Winthrobe, M. M., et al (Eds.);: *Harrison's Principles of Internal Medicine,* 6th ed. New York, 1970, ch. 357.
131. Sheldon, W. H., Stevens, S. S., and Tucker, W. B.: *The Variety of Human Physique.* New York, Harper & Brother, 1940.
132. Sheldon, W. H., and Stevens, S. S.: *The Varieties of Temperament.* New York, Harper & Brothers, 1942.
133. Goldstein, K.: *The Organism.* Boston, Beacon Press, 1963.
134. Branch, C. H. H., and Cole, N. J.: Mental disease and injury. In Brahdy, L. (Ed.): *Disease and Injury.* Philadelphia, J. B. Lippincott, 1961, ch. 2.
135. Courville, C. B.: *Commotio Cerebri.* Los Angeles, San Lucas Press, 1953.
136. Brosin, H. W.: Psychiatric conditions following head injury. In Arieta, S. (Ed.): *American Handbook of Psychiatry.* New York, Basic Books, 1959, vol. 2, p. 1189.
137. Thompson, M. S.: Amputations and artificial appliances. In Cantor, P. B. (Ed.): *Traumatic Medicine and Surgery for the Attorney.* Washington, D. C., Butterworth, 1959, Vol. I.
138. Klopstey, E., and Wilson, P. D.: *Human Limbs and Their Substitutes.* New York, McGraw-Hill, 1954.
139. Cantor, P. D.: The general effect of injury. In Cantor, P. D. (Ed.): *Traumatic Medicine and Surgery for the Attorney.* Washington, D. C., Butterworth, 1959, Vol. I.
140. White, J. C. Smithwick, R. H., and Simone, F. A.: *The Autonomic Nervous System,* 3rd ed., New York, Macmillan, 1952.
141. Myerson, A.: Traumatic neuroses. *Med Clin North Am, 22:*637, 1938.
142. Kozol, H. L.: Pre-traumatic personalities and psychiatric sequelae after head injuries. *Arch Neurol Psychiatr, 56:*245, 1946.

143. Margolis, H. M., Barr, J. H., Jr., Stolzer, B. L., and Eisenbeis, C. H., Jr.: Articular and related disorders and injury. In Bahdy, L. (Ed.): *Disease and Injury*. Philadelphia, J. B. Lippincott, 1961.
144. Evans, J. A.: Reflex sympathetic dystrophy, *Ann Intern Med, 26:*417, 1947.
145. Livingston, S.: *Living with Epileptic Seizures*. Springfield, Thomas, 1963.
146. Green, J. B., and Steelman, H. F. (Eds.): *Epileptic Seizures*. Baltimore, Williams & Wilkins, 1956.
147. Sakel, M.: *Epilepsy*. New York, Philosophical Library, 1958.
148. Adams, R. D.: Hysteria and psychopathic personality. In Winthrobe, M. W., et al (Eds.): *Harrison's Principles of Internal Medicine*, 6th ed. New York, McGraw-Hill, 1970, ch. 370.
149. Hill, D., and Waterson, D.: Electroencephalographic studies in psychopathic personalities. *J Neurol Psychiatr, 5:*47, 1942.
150. Simons, B., O'Leary, J. L., and Ryans, J. J.: Cerebral dysrhythmias and psychopathic personalities. *Arch Neurol Psychiatr, 55:*619, 1946.
151. Wiener, N.: In discussion of Kubie, L. S.: Neurotic potential and human adaptation. In von Foerster, H. (Ed.): *Cybernetics*. New York, Josiah Macy Foundation, 1950.
152. Hofman, A.: Psychomimetic substances. *Indian J Pharmacy, 25:*245, 1963.
153. Gillilan, L. A.: *Clinical Aspects of the Autonomic Nervous System*. Boston, Little, Brown, 1954.
154. Wolf, G. A., Jr., and Wolff, H. G.: Studies on the nature of certain symptoms associated with cardiovascular diseases. *Psychosom Med, 8:*293, 1946.
155. Wolff, H. G.: In Weider, A. (Ed.): *Contributions Toward Medical Psychology*. New York, Ronald Press, 1953, Vol. I, ch. 14, p. 328.
156. Dembo, T.: Der Ärger als dynamisches Problem. *Psychol Forsch, 15:*1, 1931.
157. Bindra, D.: A united interpretation of emotion and motivation. In Tobach, E. (Cons. Ed.): Experimental approaches to the study of emotional behavior. *Ann N Y Acad Sci, 159 (Art. 3):*107, 1969.
158. Rapaport, D.: *Emotions and Memory*, 2nd ed. New York, International Universities Press, 1950. (All literature references up to 1950 are to be found in this work.)
159. Burns, B.: *The Mammalian Cerebral Cortex*. London, Edward Arnold, 1958.
160. Glickstein, M.: Neurophysiology of learning and memory. In Ruch, T., et al: *Neurophysiology*, 2nd ed. Philadelphia, W. B. Saunders, 1965.
161. McCulloch, W. S.: *Embodiments of the Mind*. Cambridge, M.I.T. Press, 1970.
162. Von Bonin, G.: *Essay on the Cerebral Cortex*. Springfield, Thomas, 1950.

163. Papez, J. W.: Proposed mechanism of emotion. *Arch Neurol Psychiat, 38:*725, 1937.
164. Spiegel, F. A., et al: Forebrain and rage reactions. *J Neurophys, 3:*538, 1940.
165. Tilney, F., and Riley, H. A.:*The Form and Functions of the Central Nervous System.* New York, P. Hoeber, 1938.
166. Gillilan, L. A.: *Clinical Aspects of the Autonomic Nervous System.* Boston, Little, Brown, 1954.
167. Ruch, T. C.: Neurophysiology of emotions. In Ruch T. C., et al (Eds.): *Neurophysiology,* 2nd ed. Philadelphia, W. B. Saunders, 1965, ch. 26.
168. List, C. F., and Peet, M. M.: Sweat secretion in man. I. Sweating response in normal man. *Arch Neurol Psychiatr, 40:*27, 1938.
169. List, C. F., and Peet, M. M.: Sweat secretion in man. Iv. Sweat secretion of the face and its disturbances. *Arch Neurol Psychiatr, 40:*443, 1938.
170. Schilder, P.: *Brain and Personality.* New York, International Universities Press, 1951, Ch. II.
171. Richter, C. P.: Somatic aspects of mental health and diseases. *Br Med Bull, 6:*44, 1949.
172. Herrell, W. E.: More about hypoglycemic agents. *Clin Med, 78:*13, 1971.
173. McLean, P. D.: Psychosomatic disease and the "visceral brain." *Psychosom Med, 11:*388, 1949.
174. Penfield, W. G., and Gage, L.: Cerebral localization of epileptic manifestations. *Res Publ Assn Nerv Ment Dis, 13:*593, 1934.
175. Penfield, W.: Ferrier lecture. Some observations on the cerebral cortex of man. *Proc R Soc, 134:*329, 1947.
176. Papez, J. W.: Reticulospinal tracts in the cat. *J Comp Neurol, 41:*345, 1926. (Quoted in Larsell, O.: *Anatomy of the Nervous System,* 2nd ed. New York, Appleton-Century-Crofts, 1951.)
177. Bard, P.: The central nervous mechanism for the expression of anger in animals. In Reymert, M. L. (Ed.): *Feelings and Emotions.* New York, McGraw-Hill, 1950.
178. Bard, P. (Ed.): *Medical Physiology,* 11th. ed. St. Louis, C. V. Mosby, 1961.
179. Bailey, P., and Brenner, E.: The sensory cortical representation of the vagus nerve. *J Neurophysiol, 1:*405, 1938.
180. Vernlay, E. B.: The antidiuretic hormone and the factors which determine its release. *Proc R Soc, 135:*25, 1947.
181. Hasson, B., Über die afferenten Bahnen und Thalamuskerne des motorischen Systems des Grosshirns. II., Weitere Bahnen aus Pallidum, Ruber, vestibularem System zum Thalamus. Übersicht und Besprechung der Ergebnisse. *Arch Psychiatr, 182:*786, 1947.
182. Hetherington, A. W., and Ranson, S. W.: Experimental hypothalamic-hypophyseal obesity in the rat. *Proc Soc Exp Biol, 41:*465, 1939.
183. Nasset, E. S.: Muscular contractions of the stomach. In Bard, P. (Ed.):

Medical Physiology, 11th. ed. St. Louis, C. V. Mosby, 1961, Ch. 24.
184. Hare, K., and Geohagen, W. A.: Influence of frequency of stimulus upon response to hypothalamic stimulation. *J Neurophysiol, 4:*966, 1941.
185. Freud, S.: *Beyond the Pleasure Principle.* New York, Liveright, 1922.
186. Dunbar, H. F.: *Emotions and Bodily Changes.* New York, Columbia University Press, 1938.
187. Holmes, T. H., et al: *The Nose: An Experimental Study of Reactions Within the Nose in Human Subjects During Varying Life Experiences.* Springfield, Thomas, 1950.
188. Whitehorn, J. C.: In Alexander, F., and Ross, H. (Eds.): *Dynamic Psychiatry.* Chicago, University of Chicago Press, 1952, Ch. IX.
189. Grinker, R. R., and Serota, H. M.: Electroencephalographic studies of cortico-hypothalamic relations in schizophrenia. *Am J Psychiatr, 98:*385, 1941.
190. Davis, P. A.: Effect on the electroencephalogram of changing blood sugar level. *Arch Neurol Psychiatr, 49:*186, 1943.
191. Brazier, M. A. B., Finesinger, J. E., and Schwab, B. S.: Characteristics of the normal encephalogram. II. The effect of various blood sugar levels on the occipital cortical potentials — in adults during quiet breathing. *J Clin Invest, 23:*313, 1944.
192. Strauss, H., and Wechsler, I. S.: Clinical and electroencephalographic studies of changes of cerebral functions associated with variations of blood sugar. *Am J Psychiat, 102:*34, 1945.
193. Brazier, M. A. B., Finesinger, J. E., and Cobbs, S.: The electroencephalogram in psychoneurotic patients. *Am J Psychiatr, 101:*443, 1945.
194. Hill, D.: Cerebral dysrhythmia. Its significance in aggressive behavior. *Proc R Soc Med, 37:*372, 1944.
195. Benzer, S.: From the gene to behavior, *JAMA, 218:*1015, 1971.
196. Montagu, A.: *Human Heredity.* Cleveland, World Publishing, 1959.
197. Hirsch, J.: Behavioral genetics and individuality understood: Behaviorism's counterfactual dogma blinded behavioral sciences to the significance of meiosis. *Science, 142:*1436, 1963.
198. Weiss, P.: *Science, 101:*101, 1945.

INDEX

A

Abrahamson, 6. 7
acetylcholine, 26
acne vulgaris, 21
acromegaly, 19
ACTH, 15, 28
adaptional crisis, 52
Addison's disease, 19
adolescence, 9
adrenal cortex, 15, 28
adrenalin, 16
adrenal insufficiency, 47
adrenergic system, 11, 14, 17, 22
aggression, 3, 5, 6, 16, 19, 36, 53, 55
alarm reaction, 11, 14, 21
allergic reactions, 20
alpha waves, 15, 16, 19, 54, 55
amphotonic constitution, 51
amputation, 30
Anastasia, 9
anger, VII, 3, 4, 5, 6, 10, 16, 27, 36
anger response, 6, 7, 8, 9, 10, 11, 13, 14, 16, 17, 18, 19, 20, 21, 23, 25, 27, 28, 33, 36, 41, 44, 46, 50
anoxia, 41
antidiuretic hormone, 23
anxiety, 3, 6, 21, 25, 55
apoplectic stroke, 28
apperceptive mechanism, 44
arthritis, rheumatoid, 26
Ashley, 20
auditory reflex center, 45
autonomic nervous system, 16, 20, 21, 22, 26, 31
avoidance gradients, 8

B

Bard, 46
behavior, 13, 16, 19, 28, 29, 56
Beaumont, 13
Benzer, 56
Bindra, 37
blood pressure, 14, 16, 30, 40, 44
Bogen, 13
Bonin, von, 39
brain concussion, 17
Branch, 29
Brazier, 54
Brosin, 30
Brown, 26, 36

C

cancer, 25
Canfield, 10
Cannon, 20
Cardon, 14
carotid plexus
central motive state, 37
cervical ganglian, 41, 43
character neurosis, 33
children, 9, 11
cholinergic, 13
chronic brain syndrome, 29, 30
cingulate gyrus, 39, 44
climacteric, 21, 22
Cohn, 8
Cole, 29
collicus, inferior, 45
compensation neurosis, 31
communication, informative, 6, 10, 11, 14, 36, 39, 43, 48
conditioned reactions, 10, 38, 39
conditioning
conscious, 4, 7, 28, 35
consolidation hypothesis, 39
constipation, 11, 23, 24
convulsive disorders, 32, 33
cornu ammonis, 40
cortex, cerebral
cortisone, 11, 28
Crossen, 22

D

definition of anger response, 3
Deitch, 25
Delay, 16
delta waves, 15, 33, 54, 55
Dembo, 36
depression, 6, 21, 25, 52, 53
diaphragm, 35
diarrhea, 24
displacement, 7, 10
dream, 7, 10
Dubois, 26
Dufault, 25
Dunbar, 53
duration, 8

E

Ecoles, 3, 7, 37,
edema, 22
electroencephalogram, 15, 19, 33, 54
emotion, 3, 6, 7, 21, 25, 31, 40
emotional awareness, 7, 44
encephalitis, 17, 33
English, 3
entropy, 4
environment, 8, 50, 56
ephedrine, 21
epinephrine, 6, 19, 21, 23, 43, 54
epileptic personality, 32, 33
estrogen, 21, 22
etymology, 5, 36
exhaustion state, 52
expressivity, 56

F

facial nerve, 41
fatigue, 6, 27, 46
fatty acids, 14, 15
fear, 3, 6, 9
feed-back, 5, 26
fever, 26
fimbria, 40
Fischer, 3, 17
Fisher, 29
fissure, Rolandi
fissure, Sylvian
Fluhman, 21

forgetting, 7
fornix, 40
Fraisse, 8
Frank, 4, 37
Freeman, 17
Freud, 10
frontal lobe, 17, 40, 44
frustration, 5, 6, 8, 15, 16, 20, 25, 29, 51

G

ganglia, subcortical, 16
Gates, 11
Gellhorn, 11, 41, 42, 46, 53
General Adaptation Syndrome, 14, 52
genetic character, 56
geniculate ganglion, lateral, 40
geniculate ganglion, medial, 45
gigantism, 19
Gillilan, 35, 45
Goldstein, 29
gonadotropic hormone, 21
Goodenaugh, 9
Grace, 24
Grave's disease, 19
Greenhill, 22

H

habit, 38
Hack, 20
Hansel, 20
Harris, 28
headache, 7, 17, 32
head trauma, 29
heart rate, 14, 35
heart surgery, 18
heat wave, 11
Heath, 15
Hench, 28
Henrichs, 18
heredity, 56
Hetherington, 47
Hill, 33, 55
hippocampus, 15, 40, 44
Hirsch, 56
Holmes, 20, 53
homeostasis, 52

Index

hormonal imbalance, 6, 11, 22
Hornberg, 13
Horner, 23
hostility, 3, 5, 6, 36, 51, 52
hunger, 6, 11, 47
hydrochloric acid, 13
hypersensitivity mechanism, 20, 27
hypertension, 14, 19
hyperthyroidism, 18
hypoglycemia, 6, 11, 19, 22, 43, 47, 54
hypophysis, 19
hypothalamus, 13, 18, 23, 24, 26, 28, 39, 40, 44, 54

I

infancy (infants), 9
inhibition, 4
Ivy, 14

J

Jasper, 16
Jersild, 7
Jung, 10

K

Kaplan, 9
Kinsey, 16
Klopstey, 30
Kozol, 31
Kraepelin, 28
Kubie, 4
Kuntz, 44

L

lacrimation, 43
laughing, VII, VIII, 39
learning, 38
Lederer, 20
Lehman, 4
light, 11, 48
limbic sector, 39
lymphocytes, 14
lymphopenia, 14

M

mammillary bodies, 40
Maranon, 22
maze test, 18
Mc Culloch, 39, 44
McGavack, 18
McGregor, 14
McLean, 44
mechanism of emotion, 7, 40
medial forebrain bundle, 40
medulla oblongata, 40, 43, 45
Meissner's corpuscle, 48
memory, 15, 28, 38, 39
Menninger, K., 3, 7, 8
menopause, 21
menstruation, 11
Merkel's corpuscle, 48
message, 5, 39, 44
Metcalf, 15
micturition, 24
Miller, 14
Mittelmann, 14
Montagu, A., 6, 35, 45, 56
mood, 19, 26, 31
Morton, 22
Myerson, 31
myxedema, 19

N

Nasset, 47
noise, 6, 10, 30, 45
norepinephrine, 43, 54
nose, 20
nuclei, central thalamic, 47
nuclei, septal, 40
nuclei, supraoptic, 47
nucleus, lacrimal, 43
nucleus, lateral of hypothalamus, 40
nucleus, lateral of thalamus, 48
nucleus, lateral leminiscus, 45
nucleus, posterior of hypothalamus
nucleus, spinal accessory, 45
nucleus, ventromedial of hypothalamus, 47

O

Oberman, 16
oligemic shock, 30
ophthalmic nerve, 43
orbital cortex, 47

P

Papez, 39, 40, 44, 48
parasympathetic, 13, 20, 24, 36, 47, 50, 51
parietal lobe, 48
peevishness, 29
penetrance, 56
Penfield, 16
periventricular system, 40
personality, 33
Peterson, 11
pettiness, 25
pituitary gland, 18
pleasure principle, 53
pons, 40, 41, 43
post-concussion syndrome, 29
post-traumatic conditions, 29, 30
post-traumatic personality, 30
prefontal lobotomy, 17
pre-menstrual tension, 11, 22
Proetz, 20
psychomimetic drugs, 33, 34
psychopathic personality, 33
psychosomatic disorders, 26, 32, 42
pulmonary ventilation, 35
pulse, 16, 26, 30, 50
pupils, 32, 34, 40, 44

R

rage, 3, 5, 19, 36
Ranson, 26, 47
Rapaport, 38
recall, 6, 10, 18, 36, 37
reflex sympathetic dystrophy, 32
relay circuits, 40
repression, 4, 7, 10, 52
resentment, 5, 6, 19, 20, 27, 30, 31
resistance, 8, 9, 11, 53, 54
reticular formation, 34, 45

reticular nuclei, 45
reticular net, hair follicle, 48
reticulobulbar tracts
reticulospinal tracts
reverberating circuits, 39, 44, 45
Richter, 42
Riley, 40
Ruch, 40
Rylander, 17

S

saliva, 13, 41
Saltzman, 10
Schilder, 42
Schiff, 24
Schrottenbach, 13
sebum, 21
selectivity (selection), 4, 37, 38
self, 7
self-awareness, 37
Selye, 11, 12, 14, 27, 52
sensory phenomenon – chest, 35, 44
sham-rage, 36
Sheldon, 29, 51
Shulkin, 25
shock-decortication, 46
signal, 39, 44
Simons, 33
Smirk, 14
specificity
Spiegel, 40
spikes, 15
startle response, 30, 55
stellate ganglion
steroids, 6, 15, 43
stimuli (stimulus), 6, 7, 10, 11, 21, 28, 36, 38, 46, 50
stomach, 13
Stratton, 11
Strauss, 15, 33, 54, 55
stress, 4, 6, 11, 14, 17, 35, 54
Sullivan, 3
sweating, 18, 26, 41
sympathetic, 13, 14, 18, 19, 20, 23, 30, 35, 36, 40, 50, 51
sympatheticotonus, 11, 22
sympathotonic personality, 22
symptom formation, 7

T

tachycardia, 14, 18
tactile perception, 48
Talbot, 19
temporal lobe, 15, 45
temperature regulation, 26
tension, 8, 11, 31
thalamus, 39, 40
theta waves, 15, 16
Thompson, 30
Thorn, 22
thwarting, 6, 8, 9, 15, 17, 24
thyroid hormone imbalance, 11, 18
Tilney, 40
time, 7, 8
tonus, muscular, 41, 42
Tow, 18
touch, 6, 10, 48
tract, ventral spinothalamic, 48
trigeminal nerve, 41, 43
tuberculosis, 25, 26

V

vagotomy, 14
vagus nerve, 13, 14, 47
vasoconstriction, 13, 42

vasodilatation, 13, 16, 17, 42

W

waiting, 8
Walter, 16
water metabolism, 22
Waterson, 33
Watts, 17
Wechsler, I., 24, 28, 54
Weiss, 56
whiplash injury, 31
Whitehead, 3
Whitehorn, 54
Wiener, 33
Wilson, 16, 30
Wolf, 3, 10, 13, 14, 35, 37, 45
Wolff, 13, 14, 20, 21, 35, 45

Y

Yacorzynski, 19, 20
Young, 11

Z

zygomatic nerve, 43

/BF 575 A5S77 00001

Library and Learning
Resources Center
Bergen Community College
400 Paramus Road
Paramus, N.J. 07652-1595

Return Postage Guaranteed